After School: Is Getting an MBA Really Worth It?

Dedication

To My Heavenly Father, Donald, Lilian, Ada, Obi, and Victoria.

Acknowledgements

I would like to thank the countless number of people who helped make this possible. As you probably know, this book is heavily reliant on interviews from business school graduates a few years out of school. I'm humbled to think that they took time out of their schedules to let me into their worlds.

With this said, I'd like to thank the following people:

Abby Smith, Aimee Bland, Carlton Gordon, Diego Cepeda, Conrad Oakey, Courtney Burns, Dan Runcie, Ebony Pollard, Frank Tabora, Harold Akins, Jasmin Khan, Julian Herbert, Jun Hyung Oh, Karthik Raman, Leslie Espy, Madhavi Rao, Marlissa Collier, Nicholas Bell, Nicole Dessibourg, Ryshawn Peer, Samara Mejia, Victoria Moshy, Vishal Srivastav, Vivian Odior, Amy Mueller, Dan Driscoll, Luis Salazar, Misa Fujimura-Fanselow, and Yinka Akinyemi.

Table of Contents

Why did I write this book?

As a graduate of a "top" business school, I regularly receive requests to speak on my experience. *How was the application process? What did you get on the GMAT? What did you write about in your essays? How was Ross? What did you learn? What do you want to do? Are you happy with your decisions?*

While I did love answering these questions, I began to think that I could give potential students more comprehensive answers if I knew what my peers were doing. So I decided to start calling people. To my surprise, people were more than willing to talk to me. This was a testament to networking and human nature. ***Ask and you shall receive.***

I think that many of you will be able to get some value from the insights discussed in this book. I have pretty smart friends. My smart friends also have smart friends, and so on.

Who is it for?

Should you be reading this book? I don't know—you tell me. I envision this being appealing to someone interested in getting his or her MBA as well as those in the middle of getting one or recently graduated. *Have you researched a few options and schools for getting the degree? Are you stuck in a job you hate and need a safe way out? Are you a career switcher? Do you just want to get paid a lot of money? Are you just interested in figuring out whether you should have actually gotten your MBA years ago?* Hopefully this book can answer some of these questions.

These are all things to consider when thinking about getting an MBA. Luckily, many of the following interviews cover these questions.

Who is it not for?

While I would love to think that anyone could read this book, I understand that you can't please everyone. So who wouldn't enjoy this? Anyone who has a set image or thought on what an MBA is without at least checking it out first probably won't be moved by any of the accounts in this book. That's fine—especially if you paid for this book. Like I said, you can't please everyone.

In addition, if you graduated a while ago, this probably isn't the book for you.

Who's being interviewed?

I wanted to make sure I had a wide range of MBA grads—a selection spanning multiple schools, races, cultures, pre-MBA jobs, and post-MBA jobs. I did the best I could in a limited time. The 30 people interviewed have the following backgrounds:

- 12 Schools
- 23 Post-Business School Functions
- 11 Post-Business School Industries
- 17 Men
- 13 Women

My second year of business school, I was the co-president of the Michigan Ross Entrepreneur and Venture Club. Never one to miss a chance to promote, you could often find me pitching the benefits of membership to classmates. My roommates and I threw a number of parties and get-togethers in school, and I while setting up one day, I jokingly asked why one of our early first-year attendees hadn't joined the club yet. Her response caught me off guard: "I don't care about that shit!"

Granted, she was drunk, but her reaction was based on a critical truth of business school: Everyone has their own goals. Anything outside of those goals—they don't care about that shit. The same principle applies to this book. A number of careers and industries are covered here, so there are going to be parts of the book that bore you. I don't want you to be bored, so I've made some suggestions based on what you may be interested in.

General MBA Information

I don't know where to start.
- Chapter 3: Are You Sure This Is What You Want?
- Chapter 4: Let Me Save You Some Time

What's school like?
- Chapter 15: What's the Most Important Thing You Learned?
- Chapter 17: What Was the Job Recruitment Process Like?
- Chapter 18: Part-Time Programs

International

Career Interests

Product Management
- Chapter 10: Product Management
- Chapter 14: Did You Really Need Your MBA to Make This Transition? Nope
- Chapter 15: What's the Most Important Thing You Learned?
- Chapter 19: What Do You Want to Do Next? *Keep Advancing in the Same Functional Area; It's About Time to Move On*
- Chapter 24: Last Interview

Finance
- Chapter 11: Finance and Venture Capital
- Chapter 13: What Did You Write About in Your Essay? *Career Switch*
- Chapter 14: Did You Really Need Your MBA to Make This Transition? *Nope; Absolutely!; Not Sure*
- Chapter 15: What's the Most Important Thing You Learned?
- Chapter 17: What Was the Job Recruitment Process Like? *Just Follow the Steps and You'll Be All Right*

Start-Ups and Entrepreneurship
- Chapter 12: Start-Ups and Entrepreneurship
- Chapter 13: What Did You Write About in Your Essay? *Logical Progression; Career Switch*
- Chapter 14: Did You Really Need Your MBA to Make This Transition? *Absolutely!*
- Chapter 15: What's the Most Important Thing You Learned?
- Chapter 17: What Was the Job Recruitment Process Like? *Not Going a Traditional Route? It Definitely Won't Be Easy*
- Chapter 19: What Do You Want to Do Next? *No Idea*

I feel like there's still more to learn!
Lucky for you, I'm continuing all these stories and pieces of advice with my weekly blog. Find it at http://lifeafterschool.co/blog.

Takeaway: *Don't go get your MBA without a plan.*

The problem I have with recruiting is that I haven't done enough of any one thing for other people to justify hiring me at an MBA level. They could probably find someone cheaper instead of taking a risk on me: "Well you're probably intelligent and hardworking, but I don't know if you can do this one thing. I feel like I probably have to teach you, or you would take six months to ramp up, while this theoretical other person could probably just start doing it."

I had been debating the business school thing—2008/2009 was when I first contemplated it, and it's been an on-and-off idea since maybe 2011. I figured maybe applying would actually help me decide whether I wanted to do it.

When I got in and was still undecided, people were baffled and asked whether I loved my job. They didn't think it should have even been a decision then. I had this job I didn't like, and I didn't know what I was qualified in, so business school seemed like a way for me to gain credibility and position myself more toward tech companies and product manager roles.

Of course everyone at school told me that business school is a great way to transition. Even after I sent my deposit, I still wasn't sure. At that point I said, "I don't know what else I'm doing. I don't know what else to apply for. I guess I'll just go and do it. I'll try to think of it as a five-year, seven-year investment, and then maybe after that I'll change my mind again." It seemed like a reasonable decision to make.

I broadly applied to anything tech, and I had very little traction. There was a second-year who gave me a mock interview for a digital tech internship. I was only probably 75–85 percent prepared for it, and he just tore me apart. At the end, he said, "I get that you want to do tech and you're following your herd, but a lot of other drops have already happened. By the time the tech stuff is done, all the other marketing stuff will be. Look, there are other marketing opportunities. Check out Mattel. Check out General Mills. Look at all these other things as well. That might be a better fit for you."

It was really hard for me, because I do not want to sell toothpaste. That isn't interesting to me. I'd rather just go work for a nonprofit or a social enterprise—save the world. I'm not going to love a large corporation, and I don't want to be in a large corporation for the sake of doing it. Technology was cool because you're doing something different, changing people's behaviors, and ultimately giving something new to the world that wasn't there before.

I didn't get the internship, and I was crushed further; I needed to start figuring some stuff out. I started really pushing the off-campus stuff by looking at digital agencies. As more and more potential opportunities presented themselves, I just didn't know what to do, and I had that moment where I thought I was going to be the one person who didn't get an internship.

Luckily, the company I interned with had a corporate culture I clicked with. Somehow the interview went well; then another opportunity went well, and I was pressed again. The other one sounded like the right thing, because it was product management and that's what I kept saying I wanted to do. But the first company was courting me with this really sort of ambiguous but cool-sounding global operations role. They pitched about how I can talk to the COO—stuff I didn't get with the other offer. I also said I'd rather be in Chicago than San Diego. I did not do a good job of thinking through the things I'm going to put on my resume. I probably should have, now looking back on it.

I did the global operations internship, and it was actually great. I got two different opportunities, so I spent like 16 weeks there, which was super cool. I got to be in the New York office for six weeks and the Chicago office for ten weeks. I actually really enjoyed those experiences. The only problem was, when I came back, it took forever to get an offer and I only had a week to make a decision. The offer was in Chicago and my family was closer to New York. At the time, I didn't know anyone in Chicago. A New York start-up at the time just seemed like a better bet than the Chicago start-up, so I said no. It felt like the wrong decision, but I wanted to take a chance and see what was in New York.

After that, I tried as hard as I could to find something. I started networking, but I was still really picky. I was extremely selective by thinking about whether I believe in a company's product instead of thinking about what I can learn. I even moved to New York. I just looked, and looked, and looked.

The other thing was that I really didn't want to compromise on getting paid less than six figures because of all the debt. I just wanted to start at a manager-level role. I shied away from two specific companies because they were only offering analyst positions. After that, I randomly started conversation with this micro-insurance company in India that wanted someone to come in and do some user research: problem identification, brainstorming, figuring out pilots for them to suggest to try out, etc. That was very interesting, since I had to go to Mumbai for that work. I had a really good experience there. Unfortunately, it was short-term, so I came back in February of this year.

When I got back, I was determined to look all over America for a job. Any role was suitable, any sort of tech. I used my contacts to help me practice for the interviews, and some of my friends were really surprised that I was going for these types of roles. Yes, it has come to this. It was hilarious for a lot of people.

Since February, I've gotten different feedback that indicates I'm just not nailing it, most likely due to the fact that I'm applying to so many different types of roles. They probably think I'm impatient, or I don't sound as crystal clear as some of the other candidates they spoke to. I have a hard time getting to second-round interviews. I can do a great job getting lots of coffee conversations but not actually getting to the interview processes. Many times, it's some specific thing I don't have experience in. For a consulting company, I didn't have experience in data analysis.

Here are four things to take away in summary:

(1) I probably could have been happy skipping the B-school thing and starting as an operations associate for around $40K a year, working my way up. If I'd done that three years ago, I'd be an operations manager and I'd be perfectly happy at some start-up or midsized company doing my thing. I'd have a skill set.

(2) I think I entered business school from a state of fear, not a state of opportunity. I'm trying to keep that as a good learning experience: Don't do things out of fear. That's not going to lead to success.

(3) The next thing is not to let other variables distract you. For example, the global operations thing: Clearly I should have chosen the product manager position, because that's what I wrote my application about. I was and still am excited about that kind of opportunity. I don't apply to product management jobs anymore,

because the field is so packed with people who have legit experience compared to me.

(4) Lastly, I think transitioning as an MBA is an interesting thing if you can package yourself better than I have. I think it's better if you go in with three years of marketing experience, go to your internship, have that aligned, and then assess your options. I don't think I did that for myself. I did some marketing, some consulting, some sales, and the operations thing. It's hard to explain that well enough to come across clearly in interviews.

Luckily, the things I've gotten to do since then have been interesting. It's been actually pretty great. Customer discovery, market research, user research, that kind of stuff. It's great. On occasion, I still do apply to operations manager roles, but I mostly do marketing stuff.

Let's take a quick pause. For those of you thinking of going to business school, do you know why you want to go? If you don't, stop here. You need a plan. If you don't have a plan, don't get your MBA. It's expensive and time-consuming.

Reasons not to get an MBA:
1. Someone you know got one and seems pretty successful. This is your journey, not theirs. You can't guarantee you have—or better yet, want—the same results.
2. You want to get promoted at your company. Does your company even have an opening in the position you want? You think an MBA is going to change that? Many employers don't value an MBA, so don't be surprised that absolutely nothing happens after you graduate.
3. You want to start a business. Just go start a business right now. I promise you, it'll be faster and cheaper.
4. I want to learn more about business. Go order some books and listen to some podcasts; you'll learn the same things.
5. You're stuck and you need some kind of change. While an MBA can help this, there are cheaper ways to get past this hurdle.

What an MBA can do:
1. Expand your network.
2. Help you switch industries and functions.
3. Give you time to think about your career.
4. Help you experiment with entrepreneurship.
5. Expose you to different ways of thinking.
6. Get you to another country.
7. Put you in a lot of debt.

So many students come into school looking to escape the irritations of the corporate world. You might be dealing with too much bureaucracy. Maybe you hit a glass ceiling. Maybe your job is just boring. The hope is that life after school is different. Well, guess what? It's not at all. It's the same crap you dealt with before school. You just have more debt now.

So what should you do? I have some quick recommendations. Just my thoughts though—everyone's journey is different:

1. Write down what you're good at functionally.
2. Write down what interests you.
3. Map out how your experiences and what you're good at relate to what interests you.
4. If you have gaps in this map, take note of these.
5. Investigate whether an MBA can help you fill these gaps.
6. Ask yourself whether the MBA is the only way to fill them. Ask yourself why you need to get it. Then ask yourself why you need the answer to that previous question. Keep going until you can't answer anymore, and think about other ways to obtain what you're seeking.
7. Read this book.
8. Prepare for the GMAT/GRE.
9. Research and select target schools. Ideally they should be good at what you're interested in.
10. Crush the GMAT/GRE.
11. Apply to your target schools.

This is a high-level summary. Some of it is touched on in this book. I'll cover the details in the future on my blog.

For a head start and some structure, check out my Four-Day Career Planner at http://www.lifeafterschool.co/#free-workbook.

Want to know what an MBA did for my interviewees? Read on.

Part 1: So, What Are You Up To Now?

The quality of a graduate's first job has a large influence on whether the individual initially finds the MBA valuable or not. Luckily, we've interviewed a wide range of functions and industries to analyze recent graduates' thoughts. As an intro to the people who will be examined throughout this book, we first asked what life is like now. Use these profiles as a frame of reference for initial career trajectories.

Consulting

Robert—Management Consultant
Olu—Consultant
Louis—Senior Consultant
Jade—Senior Consultant
Elias—Engagement Manager
Amrita—Consultant
Cierra—Management Consultant
Renae—Innovation Strategist
Yoshiko—Senior Consultant

Marketing and Brand Management

Noelia—Product Marketing Manager
Holly—Marketing Coordinator
Shantanu—Merchandising Consultant
Amanda—Brand Manager
Everette—Assistant Brand Manager

General Management

Sharmila—Senior Executive Associate
Brandon—Business Program Manager
Jayden—Strategic Program Manager
Krysten—Development Program Manager

Operations

Rashad—Area Manager
Jessi—Quality Assurance Specialist

Norm—Customer Experience Director

Product Management

Tim—Product Manager
Ji-Hoon—Product Manager

Finance and Venture Capital

Liana—Venture Capital Senior Associate
Pankaj—Investment Banking Associate
Fabricio—Corporate Finance

Start-Ups and Entrepreneurship

Coleen—Data Scientist
Justin—Entrepreneur
Don—Market Research Consultant
Quentin—Entrepreneur

Robert—Management Consultant

When people ask you, "What do you do?" what do you say?

I tell them that I'm a consultant. Specifically, I tell them that I handle organization redesigns and change management-related projects. So, basically helping companies manage change based on different market transitions.

What are your hours like?

I would say probably 60–65 hours a week. A lot of how you spend your time is very much determined by you. You really have to manage your tasks as well as your time. You have to make sure that you're progressing along on all the work you have.

Do you like it?

I like it. I feel like I'm like learning a lot. The people I'm working with have been great; I haven't run into any real issues with culture or climate. So, I would say, functionally it's great because I'm building skills at a faster rate than I was previously.

What's the best part of the job?

The best part of the job is working in a condensed timeline. If I had a cushy gig, eventually I'd get bored with it. Once I get bored, my productivity starts to fall. I need a challenge to really stay engaged. So I like the fact that I get to work on a bunch of different things and challenge myself.

What's the worst part of the job?

I think the biggest issue is probably the travel—being away from my family. Not being home maybe like a week. Friday is almost a wash, because if I go downtown, I've got to commute like an hour. Okay, so you give two hours round-trip. Then I'm actually downtown doing work; the time just adds up. It makes the weekend even shorter.

Olu—Consultant

When people ask you, "What do you do?" what do you say?

When they ask me, I tell them that I'm working for an education nonprofit organization and we're trying to upgrade internet access in schools.

That's the high-level statement. If they ask, "What's your role? What are you trying to do?" I say we're focused on all K–12 schools in the country, and we've been doing it through a mix of advocacy, strategy, and now consulting. I'm focused on the consulting. We're making relationships with state-level agencies to coach them and provide them with resources and game plans. Much of it is focused on relationship building, but also consulting. It's a lot of change management, really.

What are your hours like?

Pretty manageable. I'd probably say on average 50–60 hours a week. Usually, I'm in around 8:45, 9:00 a.m. I'm usually leaving around 6:00 p.m. And maybe three or four days a week, I'll probably log an extra hour when I'm home. And then once every couple weeks, maybe I'll log on a Saturday. When I'm traveling, definitely a lot more, which gets kind of hectic. But it is expected, just considering the nature of our trips and what we're trying to do.

Do you like it?

Yeah, it's pretty cool. It's a unique opportunity. I knew that I wanted to work in a setting like consulting, where I can really focus on assessing key issues for organizations and help them improve what they're doing. The fact that it's focused on education makes it a lot easier to work toward.

What's the best part of the job?

The best part of my job, for me, is getting the opportunity to work on things that I know that I want to get better at. I'm not as good as I can be. But I have people there that will keep me honest and are willing to work with me. I knew that I really wanted to get better at the relationship management—the communication, presentation, those types of things. I'm able to do that in this job now. And I'd say the second best thing, of course, is the mission we're involved with. We're actually trying to do something to make a difference.

What's the worst part of the job?

I think the worst part is some of the frustration I feel with how I think I'm being perceived versus how I think other people are being perceived. The only other black guy in the whole company was about in his mid-fifties. There aren't too many other Latino people either. I've been able to prove myself on a few projects, but I definitely felt like there is a higher barrier that I have to cross at times, and that's annoying.

When people ask you, "What do you do?" what do you say?

My typical answer is that I'm in technology and strategy consulting. My role has been to identify how you know where the future state of tech is headed and help clients on the ground make decisions. For me, it's the combination of business school and my technical background.

What are your hours like?

The consulting answer depends. If you are in pretty high-burn projects, you can do 60, 70 a week. And then sometimes it is kind of a balance. Sometimes you shift down to lower-burn projects, where you work 45. I've had the flexibility to come in and do a little bit of both. On average, I guess if you average those two out, maybe 50 or so.

What's the best part of the job?

I think the best part is the respect and visibility that you get in an enterprise. I've had the responsibility to interact with very high senior executives, where I am helping them to drive the decision-making. They see me as a value rather than just another person who is doing work underneath them. It means a lot from a standpoint of instant gratification that you're trusted. When you come in, you have to learn something new. I think a lot of consulting is really focused on that instant gratification feature of coming in and not knowing something to the expert level, but having to learn very quickly and having to deliver value and becoming a trusted advisor. And once you realize you're at that trusted level, you think, "Yes, I made it," and now you move on to the next thing and do the cycle all over again.

What's the worst part of the job?

I think the most challenging part is that you always have to be on. Everything is an evaluation because of the uproute type of culture in a competitive area like consulting. You're always on and always expected to not be the status quo, but always to deliver at a higher level. You're competing many times, so that can change a project atmosphere. You're in a constant battle, which sometimes can be challenging.

Jade—Senior Consultant

When people ask you, "What do you do?" what do you say?

Consulting. And I say it sheepishly, because nobody ever knows what that means. But I definitely say consulting.

What are your hours like?

I used to do crisis center intervention work at my last employer. I was on call 24 hours a day, seven days a week, but it was on call because of life or death situations. So I am very much used to having to respond to emails, text messages, and phone calls immediately. It was a weird habit to try and break in consulting.

What I will say is, the mission makes a really big difference to me in terms of work-life balance. I never was frustrated with working long hours when the reality of my work truly did mean someone's safety or well-being. It's much harder for me personally to work around the clock when it's in order to benefit a business. I'm pragmatic about it, and I see the value in many ways, but I don't pull a lot of all-nighters in consulting. I frequently pulled all-nighters in nonprofit.

From talking to my friends from my graduating class and the year before me, I think there's an environmental pressure, where people feel like they need to be working a certain number of hours to prove something. What I realized my first year out of school is that I like having a life. I like sleeping. I like going to the gym.

I had to learn really quickly for myself how to be able to say, "Nope, here's how I work; here's when I work; and here's how I'm going to get the work done." A lot of newer folks just don't have that ability to say no. They fall into this mind-set of, "I must be online 24 hours a day. I must be working around the clock," as opposed to working efficiently.

What's the best part of the job?

When I got into consulting, I wanted to work with people who forced me to search for my "A-game" and push me outside of my comfort levels. I realized that that's not always fun; it's really hard. I think this is a ubiquitous business school experience. It's hard to go from being the biggest fish in your pond to being a little minnow in a sea full of other people who are smarter than you, quicker than you, and more talented than you. It's wonderful. I love it. It's what I wanted, but there are definitely moments where it's a little painful.

What's the worst part of the job?

The crazy people with crazy expectations about work-life balance. I feel like every project I'm on, there's a constant retraining of everyone around me in terms of expectations. Not just for myself, but for the team of people that I manage, and for the partners on the project. There has to be some predictability and some flexibility in the work, or all you're doing is living for a paycheck.

Elias—Engagement Manager

When people ask you, "What do you do?" what do you say?

I just say I work in consulting at a firm. When I talk to people who are not in this sector, I have to go a little bit deeper and explain what consulting is.

What are your hours like?

For the first few years, let's say that a 60-hour week was a good one. From 9:00–9:00 would have been one of the best weeks I had. Normally, I would work 70 hours or even more, because you have to travel. No weekends whatsoever, but a lot of work during the week.

At first, I was fine with it; I was learning. I was in a long-distance relationship for three years and we needed the change, so I changed my role. The position that I have right now is 50 hours a week. I get to the office between 9:00/9:30, and I'm leaving by 7:00.

Do you like it?

I'm happy with it. It's a good change from what I had.

What's the best part of the job?

One is the flexibility in terms of not having to be in the office to do a lot of the things. The second part is the international exposure I have in my role. I get to work with people from all over the world, on projects all over the world.

What's the worst part of the job?

When I was in the general consulting path, the worst part, of course, was the lifestyle. Also it seemed like a lot of my work was just creating decks and not actually implementing what I was doing. That was very frustrating.

Amrita—Consultant

When people ask you, "What do you do?" what do you say?

I'm a consultant, and I work with nonprofits and foundations, giving them advice on how they can maximize their social impact. That ranges from strategy to what foundations should invest in to how nonprofits should be scaling their program.

What are your hours like?

My hours range from like 9:30-ish to about 6:00/6:30. Some days are a little shorter. Some days, I might log in to my computer a little later in the evening, but that's about it. So that comes out to like, what, about 40–50 hours a week? It became very clear to me that I really value my life. Just because I made, like, an investment in an MBA, I'm not going to, like, sacrifice my life.

Do you like it?

I'm mixed. There are some aspects of my job that I like and some aspects that I don't feel fully rewarded by. I'm still on the journey of getting to the job that really is the job for me. Like any job, it has its pros and cons.

What's the best part of the job?

Feeling like the work that I'm doing does ultimately make an impact. I'm working alongside people who care about similar things. Last week, I went to a talk about the criminal justice system. I walked into the office and told people I went to this talk, and everyone knew whom the speaker was. We all feel like the work that we do is contributing.

What's the worst part of the job?

Sometimes I'm doing work that feels really distant from the impact. Especially when I'm doing some, like, administrative work. It's important to the client, and it's important to getting the work done, but it feels very distant from, like, impacting a person's life.

Cierra—Management Consultant

When people ask you, "What do you do?" what do you say?

I just say I'm a manager and a consultant.

What are your hours like?

On average, I'm probably working 60–75 hours a week. It probably ebbs and flows depending on what we are doing. The summer was probably the worst. From June through July, I was working probably 16- to 18-hour days for about four to six weeks. I was doing that mostly Monday through Friday; I had maybe a few weekends that I had to work, but I tried to stack it Monday through Friday when I was with my team. I haven't had a project where I've worked 80-plus hours, but that could change. I've been pretty lucky in my current position, actually. I just got promoted to manager, so I haven't had a project formally as a manager. Things could definitely change and increase.

Do you like it?

I like it. It's tough, because I think a part of the reason I like it might have just to do with the luck of the projects I have gotten on and the timing sequence of those projects. None of the projects I've been on have been similar to anything that I did before or during business school. I remember thinking that I was either going to love it or hate it. And I thought, at the very least, as long as I'm learning and have pretty cool people that I'm working with, that I have the minimum I need to be happy.

So when I compare my experience with my classmates and then other people in my class at my company, I think much of the reason that I'm happier is that my expectations were really low—all I wanted were those two things. I think other people were hoping they were going to travel to glamorous places and work side-by-side with the CEO on every project. I think I was more realistic that it could happen—it definitely happened on the current project, but that wasn't always going to be the case.

I think listening to a couple of other folks in my class who are at the firm, that are maybe not as happy, helped as well. They're not as happy with the types of projects that they're getting. I don't think I did anything different to get those projects; I just think I was open to what I would be willing to do. The only red line, I told my staffing folks and my mentor, was I just didn't want to do government work, because it's the only thing I knew before business school. They've honored that, so that's probably another reason I've been happy.

What's the best part of the job?

There are two things that are great about the job. One, you get to learn different things over the course of different projects. I've had great clients relative to what I was hearing and what I've experienced before business school. Most of our clients are very appreciative that we're there. They may be stressed out because they don't know what exactly is going on, or sometimes they're a little suspicious at first of why we're there. Most people think it's like job-cutting, but I think we do a really good job of co-creating with our clients. They never feel like they're out of the loop on what's going on, which fosters a very trusting relationship. This helps us get our projects to completion.

The second part of the job that's great is working with the teams within my firm. There are some very smart people that I have worked with that are literally two years out of college. And then my partners have all been really great too; they've had 20-plus years of experience. It's been nice to have a cross section of people with different backgrounds and different years of experience.

The pure intelligence enables me to learn from others on a consistent basis. It could be something as tactical as, "Whoa, your model is amazing. How did you do that?" and having a 24-year-old sit down next to me and show me what his thought process was.

My partners will talk about the experiences they've had the last 20 years in the media or what they've seen as evolution in consulting. They can almost immediately sense what a client's issue is and what the extent of support we need to give them is. This is awesome, because I'm obviously not at a point where I feel like I have enough experience under my belt to be able to say, "Ok, this type of project is a $10 million fees project, because we have to have about 15–20 people for the next four months to work on it."

What's the worst part of the job?

There is a lot you've got to do to get to the interesting parts of the work. It's hard to get good quality data. Sometimes it's hard to trust the folks on your team. And it's not because they're not trustworthy. There's a very natural sense of, "I can do this myself," so you could potentially overload yourself in the job very easily.

Going it alone, especially if you have other roles and responsibilities, can burn you out. I think a lot of the reason people end up leaving consulting is because they unnecessarily overburden themselves. They think that that's the only way they're going to be successful in this job and eventually realize they have no work-life balance at all.

Renae—Innovation Strategist

When people ask you, "What do you do?" what do you say?

I tell people that I'm a professional daydreamer. My role is an innovation strategist with a global designing company: to me, consulting. We basically help companies figure out how to launch new products in the market. Our company actually helps them through those processes with different thinking methodologies. We also take people pretty far along the product development process as well.

What are your hours like?

My hours are really great. They're pretty variable, but some big advantages that we have are that our clients tend to come to the studio and they're very comfortable with remote work. So we actually don't do the whole Monday-to-Thursday, Monday-to-Wednesday travel schedule. We only travel as needed, and a lot of times, our clients just come to the studio.

The first day I came in, my manager said, "I'm not a strict kind of guy. Just do what you need to do; be here if you feel like you need to be, and don't if you don't need to be." I like a little bit of structure, so I work typically 7:00–4:00, but that's variable, depending on the project and whether I want to work in the studio or at home. It's really nice being able to just work the way that I need to for whatever task that I'm doing.

Do you like it?

I love the job. It's in line with the way that I work and the way that I think. I'm pretty much completely independent. I'm the only business strategy person in the room, while everyone else are designers and technologists. It's nice to have that kind of autonomy and be able to review your thought process and go forward with it. It's a very creative and fun field to be in. I feel like I've landed my dream job at this point.

What's the best part of the job?

When it comes down to it, it's still the core of the work: getting to be that professional daydreamer for a lot of different companies and a lot of different industries. We start out with asking, "As a company, what's most important to you? What's your vision for the future? Where do you want to go? What do you want for your employees? For your customers? What matters to you as people, as individuals, and as a company?" Getting to think about all of the possibilities and then getting to actually bring them to life is a really meaningful and gratifying process. I absolutely love it.

What's the worst part of the job?

I mentioned being the only voice of business in the room. I think that's a double-edged sword. If you're in a room with 5–10 designers and you're the only one with your perspective, you have to be able to advocate for that perspective. You have to understand that everything you say is not going to be correct. There's a little bit of a dance that has to be done for you to figure out the feedback you're getting. Is it because I'm wrong, or is this something that I should push on? Knowing when to push and when not to is difficult. It's great having that autonomy and that independence and being able to really push yourself, but at the same time, it sometimes seems that it would be helpful to have a second opinion from the same perspective.

Yoshiko—Senior Consultant

When people ask you, "What do you do?" what do you say?

I have a variety of different answers. I say either strategy consultant, business consultant, or IT consultant.

What are your hours like?

I'm on a local project, so they're actually really easy. I get in between 8:00–8:45 and leave by 5:00–6:00, depending on the day. I've never been there longer than, I'd say, 8:00–7:00, and that's on a bad day.

Do you like it?

I really like it. I didn't know what to expect going into this job at all. I had no IT background. I had no tech background. I liked technology, and I was willing to learn, but I had no idea what I was doing.

I got thrown into this project, and I learned a lot quickly. I like that. I like being challenged. I like being busy. We did a lot of network upgrades in the stores, but I had no idea how a store worked and how everything transmitted back to the company. So I learned a lot of technical things, in addition to managing multiple projects.

I hadn't worked at a large company before—the amount of corralling it takes to get people together is crazy. I spend most of my hours making sure people show up to meetings, making sure everyone knows what they're doing. I feel like a babysitter sometimes. I enjoy people, so I really like it.

What's the best part of the job?

I think it's the learning and being thrown into projects that I have to figure out. I do well in that kind of environment.

What's the worst part of the job?

Being an outsider in a company. You wear a different colored badge. They remind you that you can't come to meetings at times. I feel like I can't express my opinions as freely as I would working inside of a company. When you're working for the client, you can only push your opinion so far.

When people ask you, "What do you do?" what do you say?

I work to define internal and external messaging for a B2B software product. It's my job to determine exactly what our position is in the market, develop a sales strategy, and work with the sales team on training any FAQs that could help teach them how to accurately pitch this product to prospects. I additionally work on external marketing: What do customers see on the site? What white papers will they be reading to educate themselves about the industry? What case studies do they reference to see how other customers have been treated on the platform?

What are your hours like?

I'm in a new role, but I would say previously my hours were slightly inconsistent and somewhat long. I would try to be into work around 9:30, and on a good day, I would try to leave around 6:30. I may or may not have had a call later at night, because we worked with teams in China. Those calls would take place at 9:30 or even later. Now in my current position, I would say my hours are probably 9:00–6:30.

Do you like it?

I like it. I don't think it's that different from what I used to do. Again, I think having this degree makes me more legitimate.

What's the best part of the job?

I think the best part of any job that I've worked in is independence. Being able to be given a task and succeed on that task without someone trying to over-manage is nice. That's something that I absolutely enjoy.

What's the worst part of the job?

The sense of responsibility that comes with having a certain degree. The pressure, if you don't know how to handle it, can be a little overwhelming.

Holly—Marketing Coordinator

When people ask you, "What do you do?" what do you say?

I work in marketing. I'm a marketing coordinator, and I do a little bit of everything. I work a little with students, a little with the social media, and do a decent amount of project management. I also do a lot of event planning with them as well.

What are your hours like?

I work about 40 hours a week.

Do you like it?

So far, I think it's great. I got there and they started asking me for my opinion on things, and they implemented my suggestions immediately. I think it's a good fit so far.

What's the best part of the job?

The collaboration. We all work together, bouncing ideas off of each other. It's a nice environment to be in, where everybody is willing to help each other.

What's the worst part of the job?

Right now, it's my commute.

Shantanu—Merchandising Consultant

When people ask you, "What do you do?" what do you say?

I'm officially what is called a merchandising consultant. What that means, in layman's terms, is that I am the strategist that figures out what to do with all the things that are sold with PCs, monitors, mics, and keyboard. We also sell TVs, drones, 3D printers, etc. We have a whole retail store, and that's what I manage the strategy for.

What are your hours like?

When I started, it was like 45–50 hours. Now I'm working more like 65–80 hours, because there are only two of us in this whole office and I really want to fix the business. I could work probably 45 hours, but next year would be a disaster. I have my resume bullet points of what I want to do, and that's what I'm working toward. Once I've checked them off, then that's it, because I'm not going to spend 80 hours a workweek when there are other people sitting on their asses, doing nothing, getting paid the same. Nobody's going to give me an extra star because I worked 90 hours a week.

What's the best part of the job?

It's the learning. If some of my good ideas are executed and they work, I can take credit for it. If my ideas don't work, somebody will blame me for it not working. My goal is to test things out and see what works—then I can say, "Well, I was able to grow this one category by $20 million." Five hundred million dollars is a huge number overall. For me to have any part in the strategy and say, "Actually, I grew this market with less marketing and less support," people will look at me and say, "Wow, you are really good at managing the business." That's what excites me right now.

What's the worst part of the job?

Yeah, the worst is the amount of *No* that you get. Everybody knows that there are things that are wrong and broken with the company, but there is nobody that will speak up on their own and defend a point or support one. Everybody hears from above that we need to be more entrepreneurial, and nobody does shit. They just want to cover their own asses and do the things that worked for them in the past. Because changing things creates risks, it complicates things and makes people do more work. Nobody wants to go that route. It's not about logic or rationale. It's about people guarding territory.

I'm just really frustrated. I think this is why people quit. They deal with so much resistance, and in the end, you can't do what you envisioned to change the business. I'd rather spend my energy somewhere else where I can make the business. Ultimately, I think the real success is the intersection of what makes you happy and what aligns with the company's role. If you're in a company that doesn't value what you're good at or one that puts you in a position that doesn't take advantage of your skills, you both are missing out. Ultimately, the employee doesn't reach his full potential, right?

Amanda—Brand Manager

When people ask you, "What do you do?" what do you say?

I tell people I'm a brand manager.

What are your hours like?

I don't spend more than your typical eight hours in the office. I work for a company that's very flexible in terms of visibility and where you need to be to get the work done. All in all, I'm probably putting in closer to 60 hours a week than 40, but I'm not in the office for all of it.

Do you like it?

I feel fortunate to have landed with a company that is a good fit for my personality; it's a really good fit for the things that I want to do. I've gotten to work on exciting projects that I enjoy. It's been stressful, but ultimately, I feel like the work that I do provides a meaning in my day-to-day life, which is very important to me.

What's the best part of the job?

The best part is coming up with key messaging and activation that I know will resonate with consumers and the people that my product serves. The most exciting part of what I do day-to-day is when I see all of that come to life. I work with really great people too, so part of it is going to work knowing that I'm going to enjoy the people that I'm surrounded by.

What's the worst part of the job?

I work for a big company that's not very good at processes and is also conservative when it comes to innovation. I feel like there's a lot of paperwork and busywork. It's really hard for us to move quickly. I spend a lot of time on administrative things that I don't really care for and aren't a value add.

Everette—Assistant Brand Manager

When people ask you, "What do you do?" what do you say?

If I'm talking to somebody I legitimately know, I'll tell them I do marketing. Then I'll get into the specifics of being an assistant brand manager. It's never a dull conversation.

What are your hours like?

I probably average about 45 hours a week that fluxes up to even 60 hours in different seasons for the business: business reviews, planning, things of that nature. Even in times where I am working 50-plus hours a week, I'll do that just because I'm doing a lot of new things. I'm just not that efficient at it, because I'm still learning. To be honest, most of the time, I look up and say, "Shit, it's like 3:30. Where did the day go?"

What's the best part of the job?

I am one of three or four people that run the whole business in the US. We're in charge and on the hunt for the next big innovation. You actually get to see the changes you make if you're working on something very visible, even if it's lower level. You get to put that in play and see that in execution. Comparing that with consulting, where you might just be making a recommendation...seeing your stuff come to life is really beneficial.

The next really great thing is that I'm developing a pretty extravagant general management skill set where marketing just happens to be a core capability. My group is brand marketing, but I spend a lot of my time thinking about supply chain issues, finance issues, working with the sales team, and distribution. I always have to wear so many different hats—you never know everything.

What's the worst part of the job?

I feel like the worst part is the bureaucracy. Big companies don't want to hit a lot of singles or doubles; they want to hit the home run with a grand slam. When you think with that mentality, you might not see a great deal of innovation for, like, five or seven years. Getting something in the market may take another company six months, but it would take us up to a couple of years.

If you're really innovation driven and you want to move quickly, you've got to understand that you just might not be able to do that in large corporations. I've seen a lot of my peers that are passionate in hair care and beauty struggle with the pace of the organization. But that is the nature of the beast that you sign up for.

Sharmila—Senior Executive Associate

When people ask you, "What do you do?" what do you say?

I'm a senior executive associate.

What are your hours like?

Before I moved into this role, I worked 9:00–5:00. Now I'm working between 8:30/9:00–7:00. But that varies, because I also travel.

Do you like it?

You just never know where life will take you. Because of the level of exposure I've gotten and the people that are in my network, I'm now thinking bigger. When I interviewed for the role, I said I want to be a VP of marketing. It was a goal, but now I'm thinking even bigger than that. Why can't I be a GM? I'm around all the right people now. I can reach out to the GMs of different properties. I have my MBA. Why don't I dream bigger? That's what an MBA will give you. It will provide you those opportunities to stand out—to network with the right people, to learn skills that you need to learn to be successful.

What's the worst part of the job?

The worst part of my job is undefined. It's new and undefined, and I'm just still trying to learn the role.

When people ask you, "What do you do?" what do you say?

We're in the cloud business. As part of that business, we generate a tremendous amount of data. So our goal as a company is to be able to make sense out of all of this data that we collect—about our customers, surveyors, consumers, and so on.

The team that I work for tries to answer the big questions that the company has. We use predictive modeling to predict the future. These questions inform the business where to invest and where to divest. Some tactical kind of discussions but also some strategic discussions, like who to acquire.

What are your hours like?

My hours right now range from the high 40s to low 50s.

What's the best part of the job?

I'm learning new things that I actually value. I think the work that I do is important to the business. It has a lot of visibility, so there's a lot of opportunity for learning and growth as well.

What's the worst part of the job?

We are a new team, and we're trying to figure things out. We're still defining what our role is and where we want to add value.

Jayden—Strategic Program Manager

When people ask you, "What do you do?" what do you say?

Initially I tell them that I'm a program manager.

What are your hours like?

In this current role, it's open. I have a new manager, and she just states that your schedule is pretty flexible and fluid as long as you're getting your work done. Typically, it's about 8:00–4:30 or 8:00–5:00.

Do you like it?

I think it's a really good fit. The funny thing is, they actually changed the name of the job after I accepted. Initially, I was going to be a business development project manager, handling the new business and managing projects, but they changed it to a strategic program manager. It's going to be more geared toward the strategy for the hospital that I'm working with. Driving the vision and making sure that different stakeholders understand the directions that we're headed is what I'll be doing. But I'm excited, because it'll give me the ability to work with some pretty heavy hitters.

What's the best part of the job?

Thus far, my office. But I guess, seriously, it seems like a genuine organization that truly values the different opinions and the people that come from different industries. In our current office, I think they've hired five people around the same time period, and everyone comes from a variety of backgrounds. It'll be interesting to see how we work together.

What's the worst part of the job?

I've jumped into a new industry, so the jargon is completely different. Coming from a company that's publicly held, and jumping into a not-for-profit industry is going to be a good transition. They're more concerned with the value of the patient—the customer care experience. It's going to be quite a ramp up just to understand, kind of, what the metrics are, what the initiatives and priorities are.

Krysten—Development Program Manager

When people ask you, "What do you do?" what do you say?

I would tell them that I'm like salt. I go into different organizations and do whatever needs to be done. I add the seasoning: fixing leadership styles, improving results, or changing up how metrics are measured. I guess my official title is manager in the leadership development program.

What are your hours like?

I get to work between 7:00–8:00 every day, sometimes closer to 7:00. I'm there until at least 4:00 on my really early days, and then some days until 6:00. After so long, they'll tell me, "Go home. You've been here 9–10 hours."

Do you like it?

I really like my program. I'm not sure how I would like the company if I weren't in it, but I really like the opportunity to see different pieces of the company.

It can be stressful, because it's corporate and everyone is in competition. You start wondering, "Oh my God, am I adequate? Did they make a mistake in hiring me?" But I will say, there's no other place I want to be. It's headquarters, so you can very well be in the same room with the million-dollar VP talking in jeans and a T-shirt.

What's the best part of the job?

It's so dynamic. I like having to go into different places and make a difference. They could very well tomorrow say, "Hey, we need you to go over to Sweden and open up a call center." It's exciting for me.

What's the worst part of the job?

It can be really stressful at times when you have deadlines. But I guess that's just life. I wonder a lot if I'm cut out to lead something as dynamic as my company, but at the end of the day, they chose me for a reason.

Rashad—Area Manager

When people ask you, "What do you do?" what do you say?

If it's someone really interested, I'll tell them I'm an operations manager. My real title right now is area manager.

What are your hours like?

They're terrible. I probably have, like, the worst hours anybody with an MBA could ever dream of. I start Wednesday night, and my shift runs from 6:00 p.m. to 4:30 a.m. That's 10 and a half hours. I get there about 4:30, and I don't leave until about 5:30. I work four nights: Wednesday, Thursday, Friday, and Saturday nights.

I also have an hour-and-a-half commute each way. My 10-hour shift turns into a 16-hour day with the prep time and the commute. I pretty much just go home, walk the dog, go to sleep, wake up, turn around, and go back to work.

Do you like it?

It's good and bad. My hours are the thing that I hate the most. The stress is OK. What I don't like is that I work for a lot of stupid people that are in positions of power. They don't have the intelligence I expect from a superior.

It is a great company to work for, for a few key reasons. One is the level of innovation. It gives me a great sense of pride to be a part of that, and it's exciting when we're rolling out new things.

The compensation is so-so, but their stock packages are nice. They're also growing fast. The opportunity is there for you to go out and really earn a lot, so I put up with the stress. I work these bullshit hours because I see the potential and I enjoy being a part of what the company is about. I'm happy with the opportunities that are in front of me.

What's the best part of the job?

My favorite part about what I'm doing right now is the diversity of our workforce. I work with a cool group of people with mixed backgrounds.

What's the worst part of the job?

The hours and the commute. My hours are really amplified because of my commute, but that's a personal choice. Working every Friday and Saturday night for over a year is the most hated thing I've ever done in my life.

Jessi—Quality Assurance Specialist

When people ask you, "What do you do?" what do you say?

It kind of depends, depending on where I am. I work for quality assurance for the government. If I can't disclose that, I just say I am in graphic design.

What are your hours like?

I do 6:00–3:30, and I get every other Friday off.

Do you like it?

I like it. Since my promotions, I have had quite a bit of a workload given to me. We're also depleted in workforce, so I am currently doing my "three-people job." It's stressful sometimes, but I think, for the most part, I like the people I work with. I read that government workers are some of the happiest people. I kind of agree with that; everybody's freakin' happy.

What's the best part of the job?

The people that I work with are probably the best part. When I was back in design, it was usually just me at the computer all day by myself; now it's conferences and working with people across the United States.

What's the worst part of the job?

The worst part is dealing with contractors; I'd say the worst part is when I deal with people that just don't like to follow the rules. I don't like having to be an enforcer. The problem arises if I deal with someone that would rather just make their way through versus working out and finding the best solution for everybody.

When people ask you, "What do you do?" what do you say?

Customer experience director. A customer experience director is an ambassador for a customer-centric organization. You're not really in sales. You're not really in account management. You're trying to make sure that the internal processes, systems, objectives, and measures that the company is building itself around line up with what's valuable to the end user. It's a combination of strategy management and operations.

What are your hours like?

They're 9:00–5:00. Not crazy.

Do you like it?

Now I'm more of a tactical, strategic thinker in a conservative B2B environment. I could just as easily be a business-minded pragmatic person in a freewheeling industry.

I think one of the things I've come to understand is that I'm more interested in the research, empathy, and ideation.

What's the best part of the job?

Best part is the ideation process and finding people in the organization who are on the same wavelength. Converting those that are convertible.

We have two divisions in our company: One half is doing well with an innovative, can-do attitude; and the other one has a static, non-growing, defensive culture. The difference between the two is huge—night and day. The best part is when I hang out with the group that's open to new stuff and willing to give something a shot.

What's the worst part of the job?

The worst part is when you run into a room where everybody is able to say no.

Tim—Product Manager

When people ask you, "What do you do?" what do you say?

I'm a product manager for a tech company.

What are your hours like?

Since I'm working at a big company, I have a lot of spare time.

Do you like it?

In general, I'm happy with it, because I wanted to do the product manager role. But the problems—not problems, the issue—I'm facing is that I work as a product manager at a big company. There's a lot of politics in it, and as a product manager, I want to see the market trends outside of my company. But there's a lot of politics, internal stuff. I would just like some logic in our decision-making. Some people say, "Oh, we used to do it this way for, like, 10 years. Let's stick to it."

What's the best part of the job?

As a product manager, I actually make stuff. I mean, I don't code, but I do design how this project should be. I get to work on an actual tangible product.

What's the worst part of the job?

With big companies, I think there's a lot of politics. Some people left the company, not the team. I valued their work. Their performance was excellent, but they were not getting recognized as much, so they ended up finding a job some other place. I know a guy who had a positive impact; he worked hard. He wanted to get promoted to director, but he didn't get it, so he ended up getting a director role from another company. He came back to my boss saying, "If you match this salary, I'll stay," but that didn't happen, because he had some conflict with another director. Those kinds of politics.

Ji-Hoon—Product Manager

When people ask you, "What do you do?" what do you say?

A lot of people don't know what "product manager" means, so I tell them I lead development for new online education courses.

What are your hours like?

Typical hours are 8:30–5:00, and I have the flexibility to come in by 9:00, 9:30 and stay later if I really need to get the job done. Many times, I come in on the weekend to really get things done.

Whatever the project calls for me to do, I do it no matter what the hour is. I don't keep track of hours. So my workweek could be between a standard 40-hour week and it could be up to a 60-, 70-hour week, depending on the needs of the project that I'm working on. I tell my boss, if you're going to track when I come in to the office at 9:00–9:30, also track when I stay here until 6:00–7:00 at night to get something done.

Do you like it?

I love it. I learned that I really love education technology, but I've been with my company for five years now, and I really need to see how the rest of the world does it.

What's the best part of the job?

I think the best part of the job is the creativity. I love working with the wireframing and design side of things, the user interface and user experience activities. That's what I really love diving into. I use talking to customers as my secret weapon when it comes to this role.

What's the worst part of the job?

The worst part of the job is the fact that my entire development team is remote. I try to use the agile methodology and scrum in my line of work, but I can't have daily scrum meetings to see what the team is doing.

So things that would normally take a week in a product-focused company, where everyone is in the same building under the same roof, take up to two weeks. Development is a lot slower than I would like it to be.

Liana— Venture Capital Senior Associate

When people ask you, "What do you do?" what do you say?

Well, it depends on who asks me. But if it's my parents, I say I'm a venture capitalist. They ask, "What is that?" and I say it's like *Shark Tank*. I'm the investor, you know, but without all that extra drama.

If it's the MBA crowd or my colleagues, I say I work at a venture capital fund. My responsibilities include deal sourcing; taking first, second, third meetings for companies; due diligence; and providing investment recommendations to my team. Then once we decide to invest, I do everything from the whole closing process that happens afterward with the lawyers and the accountants to working with our portfolio companies to make sure we do everything we can to make them successful. I also fill the fridge, move around furniture, and hammer the Ethernet cord into the wall. Whatever needs to get done, I get it done.

What are your hours like?

I don't have any hours. What I love about this job and what is stressful about this job is that we don't have any hours. We don't have any vacation time. I actually work a lot for two reasons: 1) because I can; and 2) because I want to. Typically, I can get in whenever, but I usually get in around 7:30–8:00, and I leave around 5:00–6:00?

That's if I have no events. I typically have an event every single night, so probably around 8:00. I would say probably around 12 hours a day. If I don't have an event, I'll go home and have dinner, but I'll still check my emails. I'm still logged in on Friday night if I have to be.

With that said, I try to unplug on Saturdays. I check my emails, but people know that I won't respond unless it's an emergency. I can't calculate how many hours. The job is always in my head, and I know that I'm always talking about it, because I enjoy it.

Do you like it?

Love it. The good outweighs the bad by far. This is the first job that I've actually loved in a long time. I have so much autonomy. I get challenged every single day; every single day I learn something new. I get to deal with entrepreneurs. I get so many different personalities. I've had entrepreneurs fucking yelling at me and screaming at me, and then I've had entrepreneurs say, "Thank you so much for your advice. It just changed my world."

What's the best part of the job?

I hate being told what to do, and I love being challenged. I go in there, and I have no idea how I'm going to do something. For example, my second day on the job, the following happened:

Partner: Go there and just tell us what you think.
Me: OK. [Slightly confused]
Partner: We need this to happen. Go figure it out.
Me: What? [Thinking] *I have to read a 30-page legal doc and I don't understand what I'm doing.*

I love being thrown in any random situation where I just have to figure it out. I'm the third person in the group, so if I don't figure it out, it's not like anybody else is going to figure it out. You create the rules. You create the structure, and you can change them when you want.

What's the worst part of the job?

The worst part about it is that I am the only one, so although I do all these great things and I go to investor dinners and close deals, I have to fill the water in the fridge. I have to work with our back office and give them receipts for what we've done. If the water's leaking, I have to find somebody.

Pankaj—Investment Banking Associate

When people ask you, "What do you do?" what do you say?

I work in finance.

What are your hours like?

Investment banking hours are notorious for being slightly longer than a typical person's. It ranges, depending on whether you're on live deals or you're just getting more pitch work, which is essentially the development. It can vary. Likewise, it varies with the type of live deal that you're on. It can be anywhere from the typical 40- to 60-hour workweek to something much more substantially later.

Do you like it?

I think it's a rewarding career. I think it's a rewarding job. You learn a lot; you learn things in different dimensions. You balance strategy and marketing very heavily with finance. So there's an equal left-brain/right-brain part of the job. Likewise, you get efficient at focusing your efforts and being analytical. I'm benefitted by the fact that I really get to work with a ton of people my age who are just some of the most phenomenally intelligent people that I've ever met.

What's the best part of the job?

It's the creative problem-solving and figuring out how to structure transactions. I love working through a large amount of different components, analyzing how I can tie them together. In investment banking or finance, you create a road map to execution versus just making it to the exit. Getting to work through that road map is really rewarding.

What's the worst part of the job?

There's always a tendency in investment banking to load up on a lot of different work, and you've got to think about how to prioritize it correctly.

Fabricio—Corporate Finance

When people ask you, "What do you do?" what do you say?

I tell them I work for a bank...more specifically, I work in corporate finance for a Spanish bank. I focus on oil and gas.

What are your hours like?

My hours are 9:00–7:00/8:00. Not bad hours. We're not slaving or working crazy hours like some other banks.

Do you like it?

It's been OK. It's not the most exciting firm in the world. I chose to leave my previous firm because, you know, it was just too demanding and I wanted something that was more balanced.

The thing about the pursuit of balance is that sometimes you find something that's just right and other times you find something that's a little bit on the other side. I think this is probably a little on the other side.

What's the best part of the job?

The best part of the job is definitely the intellectual side. You go in, and you might be trying to pitch a new idea to a company. You might be trying to come up with a solution for an existing problem, or you may be trying to replicate a previous success for another company. Your time is not necessarily predictable. You know you might use your brain in a slightly different way than you did the previous day, which I think is exciting and fulfilling.

What's the worst part of the job?

Working for a bank that has a different culture from what I'm used to. Sometimes that takes the fun out of the job.

Coleen—Data Scientist

When people ask you, "What do you do?" what do you say?

A little bit of everything. It's hard to explain, so that's the gist of what I tell them: just a little bit of everything for a start-up.

What are your hours like?

Monday through Friday, 8:00 a.m. to 5:00 p.m.

Do you like it?

It's been great, although I wish that I studied more of a specific skill. For example, I wish that I knew more programming. Whenever I talk to somebody who's interested in an MBA, I suggest that they concentrate in something that's also a practical skill.

What's the best part of the job?

It's a small company, and I learn a lot on the job. I'll do a marketing plan, but I'm also learning how to build an app on the side.

What's the worst part of the job?

The worst part is probably still needing to learn a lot. I still need to ask a lot of questions, like, "Hey, I did this; is this right? Is this what you want?" As opposed to just getting it done and moving forward without any middle steps.

When people ask you, "What do you do?" what do you say?

Right now, I am in transition. This last week, I was interviewing. I've basically been involved in a start-up, so you can say that I was, kind of sort of, an entrepreneur for quite a long time.

What are your hours like?

My hours were basically wake up, start doing work at home, do emails maybe at 8:00 a.m., show up to the office around 10:00. I was basically never working, because I was having fun. I was working all day until, like, midnight. I didn't have to sit at a desk and pretend that I was busy. I would do what I needed to do and then go read or do something else until the next thing happened.

I was very relaxed, because it was a slow process of project management. My hours were not very strict; I wasn't in a rush.

Do you like it?

It was great. I felt that I was accomplishing many things. I had to. I didn't know anything about much of the tech initially. The engineers that designed it were gone, and the construction people did not know how things worked. They were Spanish speakers, so they have some difficulties communicating or understanding my other cofounder, so they just got nowhere.

Because I was the mid-point, the bilingual person and the project manager, I had to learn how to do all of these things that I had no idea about. They were not business; they were engineering and software. I had to figure out things, be on the phone with companies, do a lot of ordering of parts, understand how systems work, and so on.

It was great; I liked the experience. I felt that I was challenged every day and that I was overcoming these challenges. It made me have a lot of satisfaction in my job. I was working with one other person, and we got along great. We had a lot of difficulties in the beginning with our working styles, but we became friends, and we became close, as you do in a start-up.

What's the best part of the job?

The best part of the job was the dream that what you're doing is gonna be something big and that you're working toward it— that you're getting closer every single day.

What's the worst part of the job?

That you don't know what's going to happen with your life. That I was not making enough money. I was barely living with credit cards, and it was very tough financially.

Part 2: What Made You Go to School?

What did you do before?

This is where it all started. For those of you with business school friends, you are probably aware that B-school students come from a variety of careers. My participants' previous industries are listed as follows:

- Government
- Banking
- Marketing
- Tech
- Consulting
- Insurance
- Media
- Education
- Agriculture
- Nonprofit
- Marketing
- Utilities
- Development
- Retail
- Consumer Goods
- Finance

And here were their roles:

- Founder
- Quality Assurance
- Analyst
- Account Specialist
- Marketing Manager

- Consultant
- Project Manager
- Module Leader
- Director
- Product Manager
- Account Executive
- Process Pro
- Asset Manager
- Sales Associate
- Program Manager
- Accounts Manager
- Advisor
- Trainer

Now, let's talk about what they "wanted" to do.

You want to go to business school. You spend a decent amount of time studying for the GMAT. You eventually reach your goal score and take whatever prerequisites you feel like you need to make it through the program. Now it's time to state why your target school should select you out of all people who are going to apply. How do you differentiate yourself? What do you really want to do? With all these different work backgrounds, what do people tend to write about in the dreaded "Why MBA" question?

Logical Progression

What I call the logical progression is the safest "Why MBA" answer out of them all. The logical progression usually involves a change of job title, while the industry, general function, and maybe even company stay the same. Analysts become senior consultants. Financial analysts become managers. Marketing associates become brand managers. That kind of thing. Many reported that they hit a ceiling in their current positions, and the MBA served as a fast track to the next level.

Robert, the management consultant, stated that he had a good amount of experience in change management as an analyst in the financial services industry, but he really wanted to explore the management consulting side of things. His "Why MBA" was focused on building his academic credentials and getting exposure to other companies.

Louis, the senior consultant, said his short-term goal was to transition into product management in tech from a previous career as a developer turned business analyst. From here, he planned to launch himself into a venture capital role, eventually starting his own fund. When asked whether that's still in the works since he chose consulting as his first job post school, Louis responded with the following:

It's definitely still something that is on my mind and a route that I sit down and wonder if I should have taken. But it also helps me better identify what experiences I should go after in my current role so I can succeed down the line. That's why I chose consulting. You can get the experiences without going directly into a corporate role. So from a long-term perspective, I think my goal is to definitely go into an entrepreneurship/VC type of space some time in the future.

Plans are great, but what about when you have everything laid out and life changes once you're actually in school? Many times, what you actually end up doing is different than what you wrote about in your essay. **Everette, the assistant brand manager,** said the following:

The initial goal was to come back into consulting. I wanted to go to school to round out my business skill set. I had all the job experience, but I could benefit from learning more about how the skeleton of a business works. I really wanted to work in a general management capacity, because that's what you do in consulting at the lower levels. That was my short-term goal.

Now, my long-term goals...I absolutely hated answering that question. I absolutely agree that if you've found something that you're passionate about, you should pursue it. However, I don't fully subscribe to the "just stop everything that you're doing and find your passion" [idea]. I think that's bullshit, so I wrote my long-term essays about what would help me to get into school. I said I wanted to be, like, a chief strategy officer for a large telecommunication company, because I worked in Telecom as a consultant. It was a believable story.

From these examples, it's apparent that in certain circles, the MBA can serve as a mark of credibility to help accelerate your career. But what about when you want to go in a whole different direction?

Career Switch

Here's where the "Career Switch" approach to the MBA essay comes into play. This is another common answer, since many people decide to get their MBA when they get tired of their function or industry. The key to succeeding in this type of essay is directly addressing how and why an MBA will fill the necessary gaps required to get a job in the industry you want to be in. The reality is that many potential MBA candidates come in without a solid handle on how exactly an MBA can help make this transition.

One of my favorite switchers, **Olu, the consultant**, discussed how his career in insurance gave him experience in managing finance and interpersonal relationships and how an MBA would allow him to make a substantial impact in education. After pointing out the flaws that he saw within the educational system from a structural standpoint, his essay walked through how he would strategically make the change to education management. Olu is currently an education consultant; it's safe to say he's on track toward reaching his end goals thus far.

Liana, the venture capital senior associate, described how she planned to go from asset management, prior to business school, to institutional sales and training to finally starting her own international dance company. Because she loved taking a deep dive on research reports, she believed institutional sales and trading was what she really wanted to do. Selling this point, she made the connection that an MBA would lead her on the right path toward this focus. Everyone has a passion outside of work though, right? This is where the dance studio came in. She was actually a member of two dance companies prior, and with dance, she saw an opportunity to make an impact on the business side of things. The opportunity was there for her target market.

Using skills you can acquire in school to change functions is a common approach to the essay. **Amrita, the consultant,** shaped her essay around her desire to bring consulting strategy and methodology to the nonprofit realm she came from. She felt like bringing in a more strategic lens to their work could really help them be more effective. She is now able to use these skills in her post-MBA nonprofit consulting role.

While it looks like some of my participants experienced success on their first application round, others had a tougher time. **Noelia, the marketing manager,** spoke about her own difficulties and how she navigated two application periods:

> *I actually applied twice. The first time, I would say it was very much a reflection of my personality. I ended up writing something about Kermit the Frog and it's not easy being green,*

making the parallel between my experiences. I had a lighthearted approach about why it was the right decision for me, but unfortunately, it didn't work out for a number of reasons.

One, my GMAT was not high enough. Two, I don't think I had proven that I had the quantitative experience to excel in business school, coming from a liberal arts degree. The second time I applied, I still had my personality attached to my essays. I wrote about Lucille Ball, who I adore. I talked about how this woman, who was a leader in entertainment, was also a boss in media production, creation, and development. The fact that you can still be in a creative role but really excel in business and own it as a woman was my story in my essays. And then, of course, I backed it up with some more quantitative experience.

As the interview process went on, I started to realize that career switchers are fairly dependable in respect to actually working in the industries they said they were going to work in in their application essays. **Jade, a nonprofit-to-consultant** switcher, noted the following:

I wrote about exactly what I'm doing now. After spending 15 years in nonprofit, what I came to realize is that there are motivated people who want to do great things for wonderful missions but don't have the business savvy to do it. So I wrote about getting my MBA and consulting for three to five years to learn the most that I could about business efficiencies and then returning to nonprofit, bringing those efficiencies and knowledge back with me.

Many international students have differing approaches than those in the US when applying to business school. Business school gives them a chance to learn more about the world's largest consumer base and test their skills out. Keeping this in mind, the thought process for many foreign applicants is one of letting the school know that they will certainly help its recruiting statistics upon matriculation. Check out some of my interviewees' thoughts.

Tim, the product manager, the first international graduate I talked to, was advised to write about the realistic goal of coming back to financial services consulting after having served as a consultant abroad for more that three years. Although this was not what he actually wanted, he felt like it was a good move to play it safe so he would get into a top school. He did eventually manage to get his personality and achievements to shine through in other essays where he described how he managed to sell independent foreign films to directors for a decent profit.

Chapter 14: Did You Really Need Your MBA to Make This Transition?

Nope

What you write in your essay is all well and good, but one critical question that every MBA grad needs to ask him or herself is whether an MBA is truly needed. Many people treat the degree as an end-all-be-all to their intended destination when it truly isn't. The reality is that the MBA is an expensive investment, and you need to be sure you're fine with the sacrifices that will be made when you choose to enter one of these programs.

Remember the logical progression group? This set is probably the least likely to have needed an MBA to get where they wanted to be. **Robert, the management consultant,** did not need his MBA to transition to management consulting from a large consulting firm, because he was practically doing it in the industry already. Robert wanted the MBA for two reasons: *validation* and *money*. A valued degree in business made people respect his opinion on things. It was almost as if his coworkers gave him years of experience even though he was honestly still junior in his career. As for money, he is doing similar work to what he was doing before school, and he's more than doubled his salary prior. Sounds pretty compelling, right?

Tim, the product manager, had similar thoughts. He went as far to say that the MBA wasn't there for the learning. The textbooks and materials he needed to learn the content could have been obtained easily. Rather than teaching him the unknown, the MBA seemed to open doors that were previously closed. Being an international student, it would have been hard for him to get a job in the US.

Post-MBA entrepreneurs kept the theme going. Entrepreneurship and MBAs, it seems, are at a direct conflict with each other. **Quentin, who is the CEO of his own start-up,** says that he did not need his MBA to get to the point he's at right now, but it did give him free time to think and be creative.

Both **Jessi, the quality assurance specialist,** and **Liana in venture capital** said they definitely could've done what they're doing without an MBA. Liana wanted to see if there was something else out there that she hadn't researched yet.

Some of you reading might think this is an expensive method of exploring. I tend to agree. With this news, you might be wondering what the point of getting an MBA is. Let's talk about some counters to these arguments.

Absolutely!

A good number of the people interviewed believed that they needed their MBAs to get where they're at right now. Everyone's story is different and, as expected, we have a number of reasons why an MBA can get you where you want to be. In this section, you'll hear from a few of our interviewees on why they feel like their MBAs were needed.

1. It'll make you more well rounded.

Some career switchers see things differently. **Olu, the consultant,** said that he needed the degree to achieve his goals within the time frame he wanted. As stated before, he had a firm analytical skill set, but he needed to become more well rounded to be able to look at problems at a deeper level. Skills like relationship management and organization were critical elements that are making him successful in his role.

2. You'll get promoted.

Sharmila, the senior executive associate, was still new to her role. When I asked whether she needed it, she took a look back at her career prior to school and noted the following:

> Before my MBA, I worked in the entertainment business, and I realized that there were just more benefits being on the client side than the services side. On the client side, you're making six figures, but you're still engaging customers and approving marketing budgets. I wanted to go to the client side and still have a voice,

manage a budget, and have fun. I felt like the easiest way to do this was to go to business school.

3. You'll learn more about business.

And, of course an MBA will offer you the opportunity to learn much about business if you think you're lacking in that area. **Cierra, the management consultant,** spoke on her specific focuses:

> *There were two goals that I had going into school, and I would've needed the MBA to do both of them. One was to find out if I really wanted to do consulting. It was all that I ever knew, so a part of me wanted to go to school to explore other stuff. Once I figured that out, moving from what I was doing into management consulting would have been hard without the MBA, because I just didn't have a solid business fundamentals background from undergrad.*

4. You'll make more money.

For some career switchers, the MBA was a necessity. One of my more colorful participants, **Shantanu**, was a former bakery owner who needed to go back to school because his shop fell behind financially. Without any savings, school seemed like a good way to get a better job that would make up for the past misstep.

> *I really wanted to do tech marketing. I was planning to transition into tech from the food field, but it's really hard when people look at my resume and they see that I was a restaurant*

manager, especially because I didn't have any skills that they thought would translate over— even though I thought they would.

There are people at my company that don't have MBAs that do similar work, but they've been there a really long time. Most of the people that do what I do have come up from sales after 10 or 15 years. Otherwise, anybody else that does similar work are all MBAs.

5. You'll expand your network.

Business school gives you the opportunity to meet a number of interesting people from a variety of backgrounds. I know I gave my network a significant boost by attending Ross. Time and time again, it's been proven: "It's not what you know; it's who you know." **Jade, the senior consultant,** added that her network is the source of her knowledge now:

I felt like I needed the coursework and I needed the network. The reality post-MBA is that it's the network that truly gets you through. I don't necessarily remember everything that I learned in finance, but there are 20 other fairly close classmates that work for the same company as me and can talk about finance anytime.

6. It gives you credibility.

Transitioning to the business world with a background in the arts can be difficult at times. In these cases, an MBA can act as a sort of validation. **Coleen, the data scientist,** who went straight from undergrad to her MBA, stated that she found having an MBA gave her more credibility in interviews. Since many colleges have regional weight but lack national acclaim, the MBA was a good backup, since she had just completed a relocation. Another international graduate stated that he would have never been recruited to his consulting firm had he not done it. Many of his friends back home wanted to do something more firmly situated in finance, but that wouldn't give them the same opportunities as an MBA grad.

7. It can get you out of a rut.

Some graduates used their MBA to get out of a hole they were stuck in. **Krysten, the development program manager,** became pigeonholed at her last job when she became proficient at her responsibilities. The company refused to move her around, so she needed something to symbolize her progression. The MBA was that thing.

8. It can be a straight path to a new career (like investment banking).

I'm a fan of students who have a clear game plan. **Pankaj, the investment banker,** stated that the MBA was one of the three avenues needed to get into the field.

> I think I needed it, because I needed to go through a thorough accounting and finance coursework. And for my particular career set, there's really three ways into it. You can either come out of undergrad, go into investment banking, outperform, and then cross over. [Or] you can, two, be working in a supplemental finance capacity: maybe you work in credit; maybe you work in private equity—and you can try to lateral over. Those people typically are few and far in between. Third, most frequently for this industry, is that people have a graduate degree and they get in. I don't think that an MBA is the only degree you need. I've seen

plenty of people with law degrees get into investment banking. But you typically have an undergraduate degree in finance so that you have the prerequisite quantitative training.

9. It can get you prepared to start your own business.

Finally, **Justin, the entrepreneur,** said his MBA gave him what he needed to get into the
start-up world.

> *Once I graduated, I realized that I could have just taken that money and started a company—learning from doing—and it maybe would've even had the same result. But the number of people, the quality of learning that I had, the networking that I've done, the amount of work I did to get into the MBA program by joining organizations to become president all prepared me to have a pretty significant network. If it wasn't for the MBA program, I would just have been a guy with an idea, and that's it.*
>
> *So it was essential to go to the MBA program to get to what I needed—not because I learned how to be an entrepreneur but because I worked my way to entrepreneurship through the model of the MBA program. I actually became emotionally and mentally capable.*

Not Sure...

Life isn't all black and white, especially this early after graduating. Some of our grads simply don't know yet. Let's take a look at what they had to say.

Noelia, the product marketing manager, worked in digital marketing for five years before going to business school. Thus, when she made the decision to recruit within the tech industry for a post-MBA job, she didn't have too much trouble making a case for herself. In that respect, no, she did not need an MBA for her transition to digital marketing. If she just cared about a transition, her own motivation would have been sufficient. Noelia felt that there was a certain pedigree that organizations expected their employees to have before they were considered for employment.

That's where the MBA came in for her. She wanted the influential title and responsibility; without the MBA, she didn't think she would have obtained them. Whether that is indeed true, we don't know. However, we do know she is doing just fine with her business degree.

When asked, **Renae, the innovation strategist,** came off conflicted. Did credentials and on-paper accomplishments really matter that much?

> *I don't know. I think that I could be in the role that I'm in without an MBA. I'd just have to get here first. I do feel like the MBA was really necessary, because I didn't do any type of undergraduate business studies. I majored in English literature and foreign languages, so I felt like I needed the vernacular. I needed a credential to ground me and make sure that other people also understood what I was capable of.*

I also really needed the time. I really benefited from a lot of opportunities that I had there. Because I did a dual degree, I actually had three years and many different opportunities to explore low-risk options. I don't think I would have been able to do that if I wasn't in school. When you think about taking a risky job, it's a very different ballgame than saying, "I want to do this internship," "I want to do this project," "I want to do this consulting gig."

As you can see, there are many graduates who acknowledge that they could have done their current job function perfectly fine without the degree. In one of my favorite responses, **Norm, the customer experience manager,** expressed his thoughts with a tangible metaphor:

The metaphor I would use for the MBA is the driver's license for business. You know what all the levers are, what they're supposed to do, and how the system is supposed to work, but that doesn't mean you're a good driver. It just means you've been instructed about where everything goes and how it's supposed to be used.

Part 3: What Was the Experience Like?

You get into business school; your deposit is paid; and all your other logistics are taken care of. You're in a constant state of anticipation as you ask yourself, "What is it actually LIKE?" You've heard the stories, but besides the partying, what is there for you to gain? Our MBA grads have all weighed in on their personal experiences, and some of the answers are surprising.

Relationship Management and Networking

An overwhelming number of our graduates stated that the most important lessons came outside of the classroom. **Robert, the management consultant,** had the following to say:

> *The most important thing I learned in school, actually, was not academic; it was how important building and fostering relationships is. Managing relationships is as important as having the functional knowledge to carry out a job. When I was in school, I was the kind of guy that would get my work done but was really there to build out my network. That honing in on my ability to manage relationships has really helped me out in my job.*

You may believe that technical skills, like valuation and accounting, are going to be important cornerstones in your education, but for **Tim, the product manager,** they turned out to be less essential. He quickly realized that he could have learned those things from just studying or taking courses online. Rather, school served as a training grounds that helped increase his soft skills, like negotiation and communications. Regularly deciding to take his studies a step further, he started negotiating phone bills, cable bills, and other such agreements with success.

Continuing with the soft skills theme, **Olu, the consultant,** stated that he actually hated networking and the concept of, "It's not what you know but who you know." He quickly learned that it was a "necessary evil."

I thought it was stupid; I thought people actually knew you worked hard through experience. No one ever helped me get an internship, let alone a job. Every one of those I got, I just applied on the website and someone happened to reach back. It wasn't till I got to school that I realized how valuable forming relationships was...whether it was seeing how some student clubs were more effective than others because of the relationships they have with the administration, or seeing how some classmates were able to get certain jobs or interviews because of the relationships they'd made.

That's when it really hit me. The work that you do does make a difference, but who's noticing you and who you can make connections with also have a huge value. All the little things that happen in school—like happy hours, club events, and football games—are networking opportunities with your class. Today that might just be the buddy you grab a drink with after school, but 10, 20 years from now, you guys are gonna be kicking ass in your respective careers. Those are the people that you're going to want to call on. That's where the relationships come in. I think realizing that and disregarding my past beliefs on that topic were probably the biggest takeaway that I have.

How to Negotiate

Negotiations proved to be influential for **Liana, the venture capital senior associate,** as well. In spaces dominated by men, she diverged from the norm to demand a higher salary:

> *My professor taught us how to negotiate through luncheons with different topics. She had a "How to Negotiate for Women," because she understood the difference between genders. It made me feel a lot more powerful. For instance, the difference between men and women looking for jobs: Women want five out of the six items that are needed for the job, while men will do two out of the six items. Those inherent biases made me really think about it. When I negotiated my salary, they told me my current salary and title were not negotiable. I still went back and negotiated, and they gave it to me. She just gave me a lot more confidence.*

How to Influence

The ability to influence others is an important skill to have, both in the corporate world and life in general. **Shantanu, the merchandising consultant,** took some time to speak on his experience:

> *One thing that is really important is influencing other people. Now, I did not master this in business school, but I was aware that it was one of my shortcomings while I was the working in team projects at school. It gets even worse in the real world. At school, people can't get fired if they drop the ball. They don't care about projects and clubs, because people have their own motives and incentives in business school.*

It's similar at work now. I'm in a marketing role that's in sales, and I work with the product, the channel, finance, systems, and retail groups. Everybody has their own incentives. I have to sell the mic, the monitor, TV, the speakers, the wires, everything. On the product side, there's one guy that only cares about selling monitors, so he may not be aligned with what I would envision for growth. He simply says, "I have my own goal." That is the hardest piece to figure out: aligning incentives so that everybody is doing what is best for the company and not just themselves.

It's the same shit that you deal with in school when you're in a group project. You have some people that care about school, some that don't. To try to align everybody to do the same level of work so that everybody learns and has a good experience—it's hard. The incentives aren't always there. That's probably the biggest lesson, and I don't know how I would have learned it well in school. All those group projects kind of prepare you for this, but unless you master it while in school, it becomes a real-world issue.

Depending on where you go and what you're situation is, business school can be quite challenging. Being resourceful is a necessity, and you really learn how to prioritize. In business school, you're involved in many things: networking, coursework, recruiting, and impacting the organizations that you're a part of. Life after school stays just as busy after you graduate.

Chapter 16: Do You Still Use Anything You Learned in School?

There's much to absorb in business school, both in and out of class. A number of responses shrugged off the functional skills taught, but many graduates confirmed that they are indeed used at the workplace. **Louis, the senior consultant,** learned to build financial models and look at financial statements. **Cierra, the management consultant,** noted that she uses accounting way more than she anticipated. Although analyzing financial statements was not new, she can make inferences on what's going on within the company based on little details. She specifically attributed her corporate financial reporting class to her success on one of her projects. Her operation core class helped her on another project.

Consulting Cases

In many cases, the actual job preparation served as a basis for learning to today:

> All of the prep that I did for consulting interviews actually was extremely beneficial for the type of job that I have now. It seems obvious now, of course, for the type of work that I'm doing, but back in business school, I didn't really [know] that'd be the first thing that I'd think of. There are different kinds of frameworks and different challenges that you see, and you have to be able to do an exhaustive process of analyzing the situation. What are the pros? What are the challenges? What are the opportunities? To be able to do that in an exhaustive, collective way requires some deep analytical thought. Being able to structure

problems and go through the consulting interview process of "casing" with folks definitely made me stronger at that.

Marketing

Sometimes lessons taught in academic environments reveal mistakes made in the real world when you graduate. **Shantanu, the merchandising consultant,** had very strong and somewhat somber views for the current state of his company before explaining what classes brought him to this conclusion:

> *I feel bad for my company because of the marketing classes that we had. Right now, I'm reviewing my notes on my capstone strategic marketing project where I talked about how you deal with a mature industry. I think that there's a problem with how we're addressing some of these issues right now. From my perspective, our consumer business is decaying, and eventually it's not going to be profitable anymore.*
>
> *My continual behavior class, strategic marketing, Marketing 101—that is what I breathe every day while trying to think about how to be successful in the market. You have to first get everybody around you on board, and there are more than 50 managers that I have to coordinate with to make sure we're on the same page. It doesn't happen overnight, so you'll always be second-guessing whether the strategy worked.*

Behavioral Skills

Chapter 16: Do You Still Use Anything You Learned in   88 School?

Statistical analysis on various data sets is a norm for workplace duties these days. Those in marketing may use techniques, like conjoint analysis. For others, the softer skills made them more aware of relationships. In fact, most interviewees stated that behavioral skills were the most valuable:

> My behavioral economics and negotiation classes turned out being the most directly related to success. I probably would've picked up my finance skills on the job anyway. The softer skills are a lot harder to learn and pick up. Classes like behavioral economics, you know, teach you how people behave...how to study and analyze people, how to make decisions based on EQ. Negotiation is obviously critical for everything. You negotiate your rent, your salary, and your love life.

It's the reason most of you came to business school in the first place: to get a job. Some people are lucky enough to follow a step-by-step process and get an offer on their first shot. Others spend months to more than a year trying to figure out where they best fit in. While there is no universal right way to go about the recruiting process, you can take some notes from people with similar stories.

Not Going a Traditional Route? It Definitely Won't Be Easy

Justin, the entrepreneur:

> It's been the most challenging and tough, mentally, experience I've had in my life. For 18 months, all I did was recruit; all I did was interview. I probably had over 100 interviews. I only had my start-up offer and one other internship offer that paid $1000 a week in the-middle-of-nowhere Ohio.

> It wasn't a good experience, but the difficulties that I faced transformed me, because I learned how to sell myself. I learned how to be confident, not because I set out to do that, but because overcoming the adversity of not having a job and having a $230,000 loan can break you mentally. You're not competing against people in Katy, Sugarland, or Houston. You're competing against people from all over the world that come here through visas or from all the other top schools. It's a very competitive world now, and my failure in recruiting made me realize that it's not me.

> Everyone faces the same issues, and I have to live with the fact that some things are out of my control. I am

happy with the outcome of the recruiting process, because it was the best learning and transformational experience that I've had in my life. It really broke me, but I came out stronger, did start-ups, and found my own way.

The reason I started my company was because I failed so much at the interview process that I said I have to make my own path. I was recruiting for consulting, because I had such a big loan, and I knew my dreams for entrepreneurship were going to be postponed. By failing to get that consulting job, I started my own path.

Coleen, the data scientist:

There was a lot of competition looking for marketing and development roles. I was trying to find positions mostly in arts companies—theaters, TV stations, and things like that—but I was also applying for pretty much anything that I saw. Entry-level finance positions at Merrill Lynch and Morgan Stanley. Whatever I was qualified for, I applied to.

Most of the competition for the jobs I wanted came from really great schools. They came from NYU, Yale, Harvard, Babson—really great business schools. Coming from a smaller school, it would have been much easier to find something if I had stayed in that area. But being in NYC, it was more difficult.

I got my current job just by networking and knowing someone who was hiring. But before I moved to California, I actually got offered a job for a boutique marketing firm in the Financial District. It was a job that I really wanted, and having an MBA helped.

Brandon, the business program manager:

*First of all, there's no way you can guide your direction
with how much unknown territory I was getting into:
moving to a new country, moving to a new city, a school
I've never been to, alumni I've never talked to, etc. It's
just a tremendous amount of unknown. Even if I had a
plan, it would have been lost, because it would be
completely rooted in imagination.*

*The most important takeaway for me was to stay true
to what I really wanted. I did spend some time, even
though a small time, prepping for consulting. In
retrospect, that was something that I did out of peer
pressure. I never really did commit myself to it; the only
reason I feel I dabbled with it was because everyone I
knew was doing it seriously.*

*Ideally, it would have been nice to be in a big company
which is more "start-uppy." Those companies didn't
work out, but I think I'm pretty happy with where I
landed.*

Elias, the engagement manager:

*There were a lot of companies that I felt comfortable
working with, but they didn't sponsor visas. Before you
even go to a recruiting event, before you even talk to
someone, the first thing you do is send an email or try to
look on the web page to see whether they actually hire
internationals. It's like another filter for you when you're*

recruiting; you have your list of potential companies, and then you filter down to the ones that actually sponsor visas.

Once Again, It's Who You Know

Krysten, the development program manager:

I think I was a little different in my recruiting process. I actually met my recruiter in New York before I started business school. We just happened to be staying at the same hotel and ended up talking at the bar. We clicked instantly. I came to find out she was a recruiter for my current company. It seemed like it was meant to be. We kept in touch, and when she came on campus to start interviewing, she sent me a text saying she put me on the interview list.

I ended up doing really well in my internship, and they offered me a full-time position. I had some offers from other companies, from going to the job fairs on campus. My school was really good with getting recruiters on campus, so it wasn't a very hard process, honestly.

Just Follow the Steps and You'll Be All Right

Pankaj, the investment banker:

As found typically in industries that have a certain tactical entry, it's twofold. First part is expressing enough of an interest in the institutions you're talking to: the culture, the lifestyle, what it's all about, etc. The second part is doing your prerequisite homework in preparation, so you can demonstrate both an interest in the job and talk to people about relevant matters. For example, if you brought up how the Miami Dolphins played last year, yes, that's kind of small talk, but you can't depend on that. You need to be able to talk about things like the stock market, things you read in the news, or broader economic issues. You need to know those things as well as any technical questions that you have to pass to show that you've done your homework.

Amanda, the brand manager:

I was very fortunate to get most of my offers following everything through the diversity recruiting route. My second-years doubled down with the first-years and really prepped us for the conference. I threw most of my eggs in one basket and hit up most of the companies I was interested in through the conference. I had a very rigorous conference schedule and interviewed with a ton of companies, so I came back with offers that I was able to select from.

Yoshiko, the senior consultant:

I think I made it difficult for myself, because I was interested in almost everything. It seemed like I interviewed for every single marketing and strategy job there was. I got an internship at a large packaged-foods company. They did everything they could for me. It was a really good environment, but the second day I got there, I said, "Oh, I hate this. This is what I came back to school for? What am I going to do? Oh my gosh, I do not want to do this job." I saw my life laid out in front of me for the next 20 years: "OK, I'm gonna manage these brands and then I'm going to get more brands." Day two, I called my mom and said, "Mom, I hate this! What am I going to do?" Going into second year, I got an offer from them. I think it helps your confidence if you get an offer from the summer job. You think, "OK, I could get that job; I can get another one."

It was still scary to turn down that job to go off and interview so I could have more time to decide what I really wanted. I was scared I wouldn't get something. But then I decided, in the long run, a few months is not going to kill anything. I ended up interviewing for more marketing and strategy jobs. Name it, and I went on that interview. I did a lot of B2B. I did B2C. Product marketing, consulting, I just tried the gamut.

One day, I see on my calendar that I have this interview for this company. I thought, "What is this? I didn't drop for that, did I? Did I come back after some drinks and drop for companies? Nah, I wouldn't do that." I realized that they had pulled my resume. I did some research on the company. I liked technology. It was my passion.

I just always thought, "Oh, I've never considered that for a job." I went on the interview, and I thought it went terrible. There was no way I was moving on in this process, but they offered me a job anyway. I didn't know where it was going to lead, but I thought it sounded interesting, so I ended up accepting it.

So far, it's going really well. I didn't plan to be in this kind of job; it just worked out. I really took the recruiting process as an opportunity to see the inside of companies I might never get to see again. I went on a lot of interviews, and I'm glad I did. I learned a lot.

A few of the MBAs interviewed completed part-time programs. The thought of taking a whole two years off of work sounds crazy, right? You have bills to pay and kids to feed. A part-time MBA may make sense in this situation.

What you'll get:

- You still have an income!
- You can use the things you learn in the classroom at work immediately.
- You can bring examples from work to the classroom.
- You'll learn the same things as a full-time program.
- You'll carry the same clout that your school's full-time MBA degree has.
- You'll have access to the same recruiting resources as the full-time students.

What you'll miss out on:

- The network. In my opinion, this is the most valuable part of the degree.
- The ability to put a full effort into recruiting.
- A life. You're going to school and working. Having a partner that's only working can help ease the stress though.

Things to consider:

- Is your employer flexible enough for you not to have to go 100 percent at all times?
- If you tell your manager that you're going to school part-time, will he or she be supportive of you? Will they think you're going to leave?

- Do you plan on staying with your current company? If so, does your company actually value an MBA? Research what happened when others got theirs.
- Does your company offer sponsorships? If so, are you committed to fulfilling your work requirement when you graduate?

The takeaway: If you like your current employer, they support you, and you have a supporting partner, a part-time MBA is an attractive alternative to full-time. If you're missing one of these, things get harder. You should still consider what you can do without the degree.

Part 4: Life After School

It's no secret that MBAs are smart, ambitious, and sometimes even pushy. As a result, they are continually thinking about what the next step in their careers is. If they didn't, they probably wouldn't have gotten their MBA in the first place. They all had grand visions coming into school, but how do these visions play out after the first job? How quickly do they transition to the next level? Are they loyal to their employers? What would they change if they could do it all again? My interviewees respond here.

Keep Advancing in the Same Functional Area

Ultimately, many people considering the MBA get it to acquire new skills in the workplace. Now that they're in their first post-grad positions, they are starting to see paths toward advancement. Here are some of their comments:

Sharmila, the senior executive associate: "I'm trying to take it one step at a time. I'm hoping that after two years I become the VP. I think it could happen if I do a great job. If I'm mediocre, then I probably become the director or executive director."

Jayden, the strategic program manager: "Within the next year or two, I'd like to get my professional project manager's certification. After that, I would like to be in a supervisor role, whether that be directly in strategy, finance, or general project management. I think this role could grow into one where I have direct reports in two years. I'm striving to use my leadership to help others rise."

Holly, the marketing coordinator: "I really like being in marketing, so just moving up in my marketing career is the next step. I'm also working on getting my real estate license to sell commercial real estate, so if I could intertwine my marketing with the real estate business, I think they could go very nicely hand in hand together."

Ji-Hoon, the product manager: "On a personal level, I am in a long-distance relationship, and honestly, the next goal is to try to finally be in the same city as my significant other. Professionally, it's to look for other product-oriented companies and then go into either a product owner or a project manager role. After that, get some certifications under my belt like a PMP, certified scrum master, and beef up my own credentials."

It's About Time to Move On

They say that your first job out of school only lasts one to three years. **Tim, the product manager,** said that he would like to figure out what the next move is within a year. Apparently, start-ups back home pay more than start-ups in the US. One of his acquaintances got a total package of $200K without an engineering background. In his words, "I could stay another 10 years and not even make it above director. I need to aim high."

Take These Skills to Another Area

Coleen, the data scientist: "Think I'm going to stick with this company for a while. My hope is to go back to New York in a couple of years with all of the skills that I've acquired, plus a beefed-up resume, so I can get a job doing marketing or development for one of the large theaters in New York."

I'm Happy, but I Don't Think Everyone Else Is

Cierra, the management consultant, said she doesn't see herself leaving consulting unless a client or industry that she feels passionate about comes along. There's always a bit of temptation though. She went on to describe some of the feelings she has when she looks at her classmates' careers:

There's always FOMO [fear of missing out] to some extent, right? There are people who have left and gone to Google, for example. They're doing very interesting things there. Of course, the natural question is, "Ooh, that's interesting. I wonder if that's a place that I could go to." But I think my experience with my summer internship is definitely what gives me pause. I remember walking away from that experience thinking, "I don't love this industry, and I don't know if there's another industry that I love enough to commit to a job right now."

I've been pretty fortunate to have had a good cross section of industries. People ask, "What's your dream job?" and I still don't know what that is. Obviously, it would be very cool to work at Facebook, but I don't know if that's honestly something that I would be in love with.

No Idea

Some graduates, like many other people their age, have no idea what the next move is. **Quentin, the entrepreneur,** echoed this sentiment, stating that right now he can't think further out than a month. Hopping from job to job is a norm in certain industries, as confirmed by **Renae, the innovation strategist,** who loves her job but is well aware that her company is a revolving door: People are there, get hired by clients, and come back regularly.

Many brand managers will tell you that the general education they get from the position is enough to prepare them for any responsibility. When asked what the next move was, **Everette, the assistant brand manager,** was confident in the future:

> I don't know, and I'm good with that. I may not know the exact block I want to live on, but I know the neighborhood. I think that's helped me to make all of my big decisions so far. I like my job, and I want to stick around for that next assignment. I want to stick around and make it to brand manager, which would take me up to another four or five years. That's where my head's at.

I Want to Start Something

Entrepreneurship is all the rage right now, and many graduates would like to test their newly acquired business skills on their own ideas. **Rashad, the area manager,** stated that he's just working to pay the bills right now:

> I'm putting so much time into it that I'm not spending enough on becoming an entrepreneur. I have several different ideas, and someday I'll focus on them. I'm thinking at least 5, maybe 10 years before I become a full-time entrepreneur.

Nonprofit

Some of our grads implied that they're about done with the corporate world. **Jade, the senior consultant,** said that she has already accomplished what she wants to do on a large scale. It's time to get a job with a nonprofit and do what she's passionate about again. According to her, "There is nothing better in the world than working every minute of every day on something that you are deeply, deeply passionate about. All the money in the world will never, ever live up to that, for me at least."

Money may not be a major factor for her, but it certainly is for other graduates—even if they see the nonprofit world in their futures. **Amrita, the consultant:**

> I think I would like to have like a leadership position at a nonprofit. I've been observing the fact that most nonprofits have difficulty in scaling. I'd love to do that type of work, but the one thing that often gets in the way is thinking about the money and financial sacrifice. Nonprofit consulting is in the nonprofit sector but is much better paid than working in a nonprofit. So that would be my ideal path, but when reality sinks in, I may have to rethink that.

Go International

What happens when you're comfortable in your position and you're looking for a challenge? A change of scenery might be necessary. **Amanda, the brand manager:**

> I've really started to get my stride with my career. There's a little bit of trying to figure out, like, where my place in the world is in terms of where I

want to settle down. At the same time, I'm contemplating doing an international stint— picking a country and going to work locally there for a short bit of time. I see myself doing marketing for a little while longer— actually for a lot while longer.

Chapter 20: What Advice Would You Give Yourself If You Could Do It Again?

So you've finished B-school. You had the time of your life. You're older and more experienced. If you could go back in time and give yourself advice, what would you tell yourself? How would you have optimally spent your time?

Focus

Tim, the product manager: "You need to know what you want to get out of an MBA and what you want to do after it. I didn't have that picture. I got in, and I started interviewing all these different companies: I interviewed for a pharmaceutical company; I interviewed with with a credit card company; I interviewed with an oil company. I just interviewed in every different industry, because I wasn't sure what I wanted to do. They knew that I wasn't really interested in their companies, so I was not getting enough offers. I did some soul searching and thought about what I really wanted to do. I wanted to come back to tech and become product manager again."

Don, the market research consultant: "When you're there, don't get distracted by anything. By city, by what the company does...just think about what skills you want to learn while you are in school, your internship, and any other side projects."

Jade, the senior consultant: "Not to get caught up in the noise. Everyone is at business school for a different reason. I did a lot of peer coaching; I did a lot of career counseling while I was at school. It was interesting to see people who would come in thinking, "Here's what I want to do," and then inevitably end up applying for consulting or iBanking because that's where all the money is.

"The one thing I said to people over and over again is, 'You need to understand what you're hoping to get out of this and stick with that. Getting some job where you'll never see your friends and family, but earn a lot of money that you'll never have time to spend, might not be what's best for you.' I felt like I did a great job of balancing that out over time, but there were definitely moments in my MBA experience that I lost sight of that a little bit."

Renae, the innovation strategist: "I think that one of the big lessons is learning when to walk away from things. When I came into B-school, I felt like I had a lot to prove because I didn't have a business background. So when I took on a challenge, I felt like I had to hang on to it, take it all the way through. There were a couple incidences where things were just not worth the time."

"I guess more planning. A lot of people think of just saying, 'All right, I'll get this MBA and then

I'll get this job.' It just doesn't work like that. That's a changing paradigm with us millennials. We thought that you get a college degree, get a good job, and you're done. I think you have to be more practical and think, 'OK, within the first year or so of the MBA, I should have already planned out the kind of companies that I wanted to work for, or this industry that I wanted to be in.'

"I had a soft interest in health care, but I didn't have any tangible leads on how to actually enter that industry. The value of networking helped me out, because I was able to talk to people that had their hands in other areas; I could kind of latch on to them and work my way in. But I think having more of a plan of what I wanted to do long-term would have helped. "

Believe in Myself

Liana, the venture capital senior associate: "A lot of crying happened. I would take my GMAT and I wouldn't get the score I want. I took the GMAT four or five times. I was applying and saying, 'I'm not gonna get in,' and, 'What am I doing with my life?' My advice would be to tell myself to shut the fuck up and just do it—things are gonna work out.

"I had to go through all this stuff to appreciate what I'm doing now. Right now, I'm 31 years old, so I'd ask myself, 'Am I too old? Am I still having kids? If I have kids, I'm going to have to leave VC, and I don't want to.' I've been with my boyfriend for five years, and everyone asks,

'Are you guys gonna get married?' We're off doing our own thing, but it gets a lot harder to have kids, so if you want them, you've got to start having them now."

Noelia, the product marketing manager: "Don't feel bad if you don't get an on-campus job. I was really focused on getting an on-campus position...you know, the Amazons of the world and the Microsofts of the world. I started looking at some start-ups and maybe some more nontraditional paths a little later."

Everette, the assistant brand manager: "I would say, 'You're smarter than you think you are. You're more confident than you think you are. You've already got good instinct and good judgment. Just continue to be who you are, but understand that at the end of the day, as long as you believe in yourself, other people will believe in you as well.'"

Krysten, the development program manager: "If I could go back in time, I would probably go way back before college or business school and tell my little girl self that it's OK to be different. Honestly embracing the fact that I was different was what helped me get where I am today."

Rashad, the area manager: "Self-realization. Know who you are and don't have to change for anyone else. If your company doesn't see your value, take it to someone who will. You're not going to gain true wealth by working for someone else anyway."

Yoshiko, the senior consultant: "I'd say, 'Don't worry so much.' Before business school, each step of the way, I was worried about stuff that hadn't happened. 'OK, what if I get into this school; how am I going to move there?' Then once I was at school, it was, 'What if I don't get an internship?' I wasted a lot of time thinking about things that might never happen."

Take a Chance

Louis, the senior consultant: "If I could step back in time, I would tell myself, 'Don't be so careful. Be open to taking a little bit more risk. Push to learn the things that you want to learn.' For instance, with entrepreneurship, I got to a certain level and stopped. Now I wished I would have pushed a little bit harder. That was my initial route coming into business school."

Don, the market research consultant: "Quit your job right now and see what else you can find while you are applying. If you find something that you are happy doing, then defer for a year and see if you are happy for a year."

Cierra, the management consultant: "I think I would have probably encouraged myself to take a little bit more risk. I was so focused on what I would learn in the classroom that there were some things that I didn't take advantage of. I wish I had done something like our student venture funds or the social impact challenges. I think those are the ones I shied away from because I didn't think that I'd be good at them. I probably don't need it for my job right now anyway, but I think it would have rounded out the perspective I brought to projects. I would have gladly sacrificed some of the classroom time to do these things."

Fabricio, in corporate finance: I listened to the advice, but I didn't execute it 100 percent; I probably executed it 75 percent. I would say, 'Be bold—don't be afraid of failure.' It's a smart person's problem. When you have good options, you tend to see your downside risk. To somebody who has nothing to lose, they're going to go full in. They have no backup. They work hard. They kick butt. They make certain decisions like there's no backup.

I feel like people with a lot of like good options get spoiled and are not that aggressive. So I think if I could go back to my younger self, I would probably be a little bit bolder and take a few more risks."

Make the Best Use of Your Time

Brandon, the business program manager: "Managing time is probably the most important thing I could imagine. A lot of times, you do things just because others are doing it. Do as little as you can—as little as you want—and don't be your own enemy by not respecting your free time. Keep your free time to yourself; engage in things which you actually like. If you like to sing, go sing. Use the time to do what you want and not do another case competition. The ROI on those things is small."

Ji-Hoon, the product manager: "I would say, 'When it comes to school, manage your time very wisely. Do not procrastinate on a project until the last two, three days, because you will be doing some last-minute crunch time and some late nights. Really space it out.'

"On the professional side, start building your resume immediately, right after your MBA is over. After that, put it out there. My mistake was to not advertise myself until I'm done with my MBA. I think that hurt myself in the long run. I was honestly too scared to rock the living and work situation at the time. My job is very flexible and accommodating. I was afraid that nobody else would be. On the contrary, I was very surprised how many people would be willing to and how much I hurt my chance to have something better lined up once I graduated. So I would tell myself to be more aggressive as I neared completion of my degree."

Robert, the management consultant: "I would tell myself [to] study hard, quite frankly, because a lot is expected of you as an MBA. The best way to be preparing for that is to really give it your all in school."

Quentin, the entrepreneur: "I wish I learned more of the financial stuff."

Sharmila, the senior executive associate: "I would cut all the social stuff. I would spend 30 percent less of time doing the club and the social activities and more on actually learning and studying, trying to really broaden my knowledge. The expectation in the corporate world is that since you have your MBA, you know a lot more than what you actually do."

Travel

Robert, the management consultant: "Go travel out of the country while you're here. I should have done that. I had an opportunity to do it right after first year, and I didn't."

Amanda, the brand manager: "I'd say definitely travel more during business school—forget about the loans."

Robert, the management consultant: "I would challenge myself to take a new venture creation class. I actually have an idea now, but I'm going to be doing a lot more research on how to start a venture, because I didn't take the class."

Skip the MBA

Jessi, the quality assurance specialist: "I don't know, it's probably not worth it. I think I could have 'found myself' by going to a different school for my MBA. I went to my part-time program mainly because they offered the day classes. That was awesome. I probably would never have wanted to do it if I couldn't do it during work or during the day. I felt like they were giving MBAs out to whoever would pay for a class. I think I could've gotten more out of it somewhere else, but then again, I don't know if it would've mattered."

A Message to the Foreign Students: Network More

Tim, the product manager: "Some foreign students spend most of their time studying business cases to catch up with the schoolwork, because it takes longer to read the materials. If you don't do any networking, that's not smart. I think you need to prioritize what you want to get out of this and what you want to do."

Keep an Open Mind

Shantanu, the merchandising consultant: "Understand where people are coming from and come up with a solution for how to solve a problem rather than saying no, shutting the door, and not being cooperative. I think that's key going into business school and the workplace. People have ideas, and others immediately say, 'No, why? Who would buy that?' Sometimes I don't realize I might not say no right off, but I give a negative response. Rather, it should [come] from a position of, 'Let's figure out how to make this a reality. What would it take from a rational mind-set?'"

Get Some More Experience

Coleen, the data scientist: "I'd probably work for a year or two before going right into the MBA. I think I would have been more appealing to hiring managers if I had some practical work experience, as opposed to high school, undergrad, grad school, all in a row."

If you just graduated, listen up! Our MBAs have advice for you. If you're a few years out, pay attention as well. There are some key insights here.

Everything Will Be Fine

Krysten, the development program manager: "Just enjoy. I got so worried and stressed about entering the workforce. I was thinking about my student loan kicking in, promotions, etc. I needed to enjoy the fact that I was in school amongst my peers and I came through two really rough years. I'd tell myself to spend that money in my account. I'll earn it back. Go on that vacation; get myself a massage. If I could send myself a note, it would be, 'Chill.'"

Justin, the entrepreneur: "I have accomplished my life dream, which was to go to my alma mater. My failures in recruiting have nothing to do with my success. My failure in my start-up during school wasn't a reflection on who I was. I'd tell myself that I was successful and I had to go through very hard times to realize that I actually was happy. So I would tell myself, 'Open your eyes; you're actually in a good place in your life; and you're not in this miserable, bad position that you think you are.'"

Coleen, the data scientist: "I would tell myself not to settle, negotiate for what I want, and hold on to it for a year or two. The job you have right out of college isn't going to be forever."

Aim Higher

Holly, the marketing coordinator: "When I was about to graduate, I was very comfortable at my part-time job. It was a great place to work, but I think I should have pushed myself a little more and gotten a job that was going to further my career more quickly. Something outside of my comfort zone."

You Can Leave

Amrita, the consultant: "I would tell myself not be afraid to quit, which may not sound like the responsible answer. Looking back now, it's fine to leave a job if it's not a good fit."

Enjoy Life

Fabricio, in corporate finance: "Enjoy the moment, and enjoy life a little bit more. Don't get caught up with the job search or work process.

Chapter 21: What Advice Would You Give Yourself at 117 Graduation?

"I think a lot of people who are coming out of business school are just 100 percent consumed in their job and their new life. You tend to forget everything else around you: friends, important events, girlfriend. You're focusing 100 percent on your job, and within the first two, three years we're out of that job anyway."

Chapter 21: What Advice Would You Give Yourself at 118 Graduation?

I also took the time to pick my interviewees' brains on what books they were reading. Where do our MBAs get their knowledge?

1984 by George Orwell
A Tale of Two Cities by Charles Dickens
Ahead of the Curve by Philip Delves Broughton
Between the World and Me by Ta-Nehisi Coates
Communist Manifesto by Karl Marx and Friedrich Engels
Daring Greatly by Brené Brown
Disciplined Entrepreneurship by Bill Aulet
Freakonomics by Steven D. Levitt and Stephen J. Dubner
Give and Take by Adam Grant
Grain Brain by David Perlmutter
Hardwiring Excellence: Purpose, Worthwhile Work, Making a Difference by Quint Studer
How to Dream: A Guide to an Extraordinary Life by Umair Haque
Into Thin Air by Jon Krakauer
Investing in your 20s and 30s for Dummies by Eric Tyson
Just Mercy by Bryan Stevenson
Lean In by Sheryl Sandberg
Made to Stick by Chip Heath and Dan Heath
Mindset: The New Psychology of Success by Carol Dweck
Misbehaving: The Making of Behavioral Economics by Richard Thaler
Modern Romance by Aziz Ansari
Money: Master the Game by Tony Robbins
Rising Strong by Brené Brown
Saving Capitalism: For the Many, Not the Few by Robert B. Reich
Team of Teams: New Rules of Engagement for a Complex World by General Stanley McChrystal

The Alchemist by Paulo Coelho
The Art of Spelling: The Madness and the Method by Marilyn vos Savant
The Black Male Handbook by Kevin Powell
The Elements of Style by William Strunk Jr.
The First 90 Days by Michael D. Watkins
The Magicians by Lev Grossman
The Souls of Black Folks by W.E.B. Du Bois
The Wealth of Nations by Adam Smith

At the end of the day, this is the question that every potential MBA candidate wants answered and every MBA graduate asks him or herself.

Absolutely

Robert, the management consultant: "For me specifically, it was well worth it. I got a scholarship, so I didn't have to pay tuition. It was basically like a $40–45,000 investment in my future. I paid, like, 32 grand to get my undergrad degree, so for me to get such a big increase in salary, it was well worth it."

Sharmila, the senior executive associate: "All in all, it was definitely was. I'm in a program with other like-minded people. We have access to high-level executives. There's nothing I regret about going to business school. What I would have done differently is make myself more well rounded in the classes I took."

Jade, the senior consultant: "Yes, absolutely. I feel like a number of people who I talk to went to school specifically to get a skill set for a particular job. I wanted to learn about business so that I could apply it to something different. It wasn't a 'two plus two equals four' thing. I wanted to understand the world, understand the environment, and understand how to navigate it so I could benefit something that I'm passionate about. I feel like I got that out of it. I know a number of people who graduated, got the job they wanted, and then realized that it's not very fulfilling. I didn't have that problem."

Renae, the innovation strategist: "It's a definite yes. I did get the technical education that I needed, but I also made so many really close friends. I think some of my business school friends are closer friends than the ones I grew up with. Finally, it gave me that room to explore. Prior to business school, I wasn't comfortable taking risks, because I felt like there was so much riding on it. Now after business school, having seen a lot of those risks pay off well, and I'm much more comfortable taking big risks."

Everette, the assistant brand manager: "Absolutely—it was worth every single penny that I'm in debt for right now. It was literally the most transformative experience I've had to date from a personal development, global exposure, and a pure networking standpoint. I don't really think you can put a price tag on that."

Coleen, the data scientist: "Definitely. It gave me many well-rounded skills. Being a liberal arts major, if I were going into a more traditional business job, I don't think I would have had the same credibility."

Krysten, the development program manager: "Definitely. I came out with a student loan that I'm gonna be paying for the next 10 years. That's the downside of it, but the upside is dramatically increasing my earning potential. So although I'm paying money back for this degree, that 10 years will go by and I'll get to enjoy the money."

Rashad, the area manager: "Yeah, I've had a lot of value in it. As an engineer, you're trained how to think and problem solve, which is a great tool to have. I think the business degree really compliments engineering well. Understanding the business piece is the thing that makes you dangerous. If you already have the skill set to be good, make changes, and improve, the addition of business savvy and knowledge to turn those things into dollar signs makes you dangerous.

"I think I would probably give the engineering degree more weight, but I guess at the end of the day, the business piece is what's going to pay off."

Ji-Hoon, the product manager: "One hundred percent worth it. It helped me be more versatile. I know more about how the world of business works, and it definitely made me more marketable for the jobs I'm interested in. It definitely was worth it for me, because I was changing careers."

Pankaj, the investment banking associate: "Could I do what I do without it? No, not at all. Did I learn a ton? Absolutely. Did I develop and grow intellectually because of it? For sure. Did it put me on a path that I really wanted to pursue that I wouldn't have been able to pursue without it? Entirely.

"For example, if you want to go into corporate strategy, but you're an engineer, then you're going to need an MBA. If you want to get into progressive banking, but you're a strategy guy, you're going to need your MBA. If you want to go into product marketing, but you spent five years in the military, you need an MBA. That's the reality. In all three of those examples is, each of those three people is insufficient in their current capabilities, so they need to go get that education to compete at that next level. So I do not think an MBA creates an advantage. What I think it does is, it creates an opportunity to close a disadvantage.

"It is 100 percent possible for me to do what I do without an MBA. Do you need an MBA to be successful? Not a chance. In fact, the most successful people typically don't have an MBA, because they're already strong enough not to need it."

I'm Not Sure

Don, the market research consultant: "I don't think I really have an answer, because I think a lot of it is going to depend on, where will I land for the next couple of years? How does that compare to what I think I could've done had I not gone to business school? If I just end up at an analyst sort of role at a company that I'm not excited about, then I'd probably give it a thumbs-down. If I get into an exciting place where I'm learning, then maybe it would be a thumbs-up.

"Right now, the most I can say is that I think I probably made some missteps, but in terms of learning, I think actually I really enjoyed business school. Not just the socializing either. I feel like I gave myself a good indirect business education, because I worked at a start-up as well as a consulting engagement right before school. I knew some things about business broadly, but school really filled in the gaps. I learned so much.

"But, I think going to business school helped me meet a community of people with a business background who care about things. That was something I was excited to have; my community before school didn't have that. Now whether it was worth the cost—that one's a really hard one for me to answer. I don't know if I could answer that, honestly. The experience itself was great. The people I met were awesome. The actual landing on my feet hasn't gone well, so for now I have to give you a question mark."

Jayden, the strategic program manager: "I think it's a hard question to answer. When I graduated, I didn't get a pay raise. I think what it does is, it allows [you] to enter into a different market of not only advancement but also professionalism. I was in a position where I still needed to learn a little bit more. I needed to have some more business experience. So yeah, I definitely think it's worth it. Should it be as expensive as it is? Probably not."

Holly, the marketing coordinator: "I think it was. I gained a lot of knowledge being one of the younger ones in my class. Being fresh out of school made it a little bit easier than all of the other people in my class who had been out of school for a while."

Norm, the customer experience manager: "I'll tell you in a couple of years."

Part 5: Let's Wrap This Up

So we've heard from 30 different graduates on their experiences before, during, and after school. By this time, you should have enough to point yourself in the right direction. I do have one more interview candidate though: me. This one is for tech product managers and entrepreneurs though. If this isn't your interest, you may want to skip the next chapter.

As I approach finishing this book, I realize that I myself am a year out of school as well. Thus, I thought it would be pretty interesting to turn the tables and ask myself the same questions I've been asking everyone else. This is an engineer, product manager, and aspiring entrepreneur's view, so use that frame of mind as you read my answers.

When people ask you, "What do you do?" what do you say?

I always say I'm a product manager for a small software company. If they follow up by asking what that means, I tell them I do whatever it takes to get products out of development and into customers' hands. That means anything from creating marketing material to coding, if needed.

What did you do before school?

Before school, I was an embedded software engineer and a product manager. I've done development, but my first role after school was primarily in testing. I landed the product manager position by chance when my team went through a rapid transition, leaving the position open for me to do it temporarily as a stopgap till we found a replacement. It soon became my full-time role.

Fast forward a year and a half, and you find me in one of the most depressing periods of my life up to that time. For at least half a year, I wanted to get fired every morning. Truly hating your job is one of the worst things you can experience in the "developed" world. Think about it. You spend anywhere from 40–80 hours a week at work. That's anywhere from 24–48 percent of your week. Would you really want misery to be prominent in that much of your life?

This is not to say that I worked for a bad company. It was actually a great company overall. There were just too many questionable decisions made at levels higher than my own for my taste. By the time direction trickled down to the minions, it was either too late or there was too much bureaucracy in place to make changes. It became difficult to stay motivated when your opinion was never taken into account, even though you're the one building the products.

What did you write about in your business school application essay?

I wrote about my path to my long-term goal of creating schools in Nigeria for math and science. While I was researching the pros and cons of business school, I became intensely interested in entrepreneurship. The plan was to become a serial entrepreneur, most likely in the tech space, and use the wealth generated from those businesses to build the schools. I wanted to work for a smaller company that would give me a great amount of responsibility to increase my skill set and prepare myself for the tasks that were at hand.

I'm a product manager for a small tech company right now, so I think things are going as planned so far.

Do you think you really needed your MBA to do this? Why or why not?

Not at all. During my second term of my first year, I came to the realization that if you want to be an entrepreneur, you should just go ahead and do it. No amount of school is going to teach you how to keep pushing when your bills are due and you're out of money. You just have to jump in.

Around the same time, I realized that I still wanted to be as close to engineering as possible. In my eyes, product management was the closest job to engineering that an MBA could get. As far as product management goes, I could definitely do many of the things I do at work today without my business degree. Everything that I learned in school could have been picked up reading a few books. What would have been harder to acquire is the network that I have now.

Do you still use anything you learned in school?

Surprisingly, I do. In my year post business school, I've used the informal network analysis, discounted cash flow analysis, logistical regression, and sentiment and data analysis in both work and personal projects.

What's the most important thing you learned in school?

Team diversity truly results in a better product and outcome. I think it's pretty comical that it took business school for me to realize this when I'm a black male in the tech industry. I remember the exact moment it hit me too.

We were assigned a group for all of our assignments in our core marketing class. By this time in the year, we were fairly familiar with each other as classmates, so there was no fear of hurting feelings if opinions differed. Eager to prove to myself that marketing was something that I could indeed stomach, I tackled our second assignment with a well-thought-out answer that I believed was the spot-on solution to the problem at hand.

I confidently presented my solution to the rest of the team. One of my partners agreed with my thoughts, but another had different plans. After I was done, she proceeded to thoroughly dismantle all of my points. It was all in a tactful manner, but I can admit that I wasn't ecstatic about it. How was I so off? How did I miss so many clear holes in my analysis? I had team members who agreed with me; I couldn't have been that wrong.

That's when it really hit me: She had a completely different perspective from my own. In an attempt to make my thinking as efficient as possible, it seemed like my brain had blocked out other reasonable solutions, choosing to focus on what I knew. Imagine if my team was completely full of people just like me. We would have all come to the same completely wrong conclusion.

This was when I realized the importance of having a team with diverse backgrounds. You get a mix of people who can check each other's ideas when they don't quite measure up. Everyone benefits at the end of the day.

What are your hours like?

I probably work an average of 50 hours a week. Pretty good for a post-MBA job, right? When I was recruiting for my post-graduation job, I specifically said that one of my criteria was that I have to be in the 40- to 60-hour range in order to have free time for my personal projects. I made it a point to ask how many hours each person I interviewed with worked.

How are you liking it so far?

I really enjoy my job. It's a small company, so I've been given a good amount of responsibility for someone who has a tech background but was unfamiliar with the industry. It's rewarding to be in an environment where people trust you with the business, especially after being in a giant company prior to school. When you combine that with the opportunity to work with some pretty smart people, it's a compelling package.

What's the best part of the job?

It's the variety of the work that I have to do. Like I said before, I work for a small company, so I have to wear many hats as a product manager. I always say I have self-diagnosed ADHD, so being forced to flip back and forth between various tasks and strategies suits me just fine.

What's the worst?

Marketing. Anyone who knows me knows I can't stand marketing. I understand it all. I can communicate with marketing and tell them how to position a product. What I hate to do is tactically executing the marketing strategies. Whenever I have to help do this, I drag my feet.

Do you have any funny or interesting work stories you don't mind telling?

I'm a huge rap and hip-hop fan, so naturally I have a large selection that I listen to in my car. I certainly have a "Parental Discretion Advised" taste in music. One day when a business partner came for an on-site visit, I drew the short straw for the day and had to drive to a nearby restaurant for a work lunch.

I hop in the car and pull up on my coworkers waiting for a ride. As I pull off, they notice, unbeknownst to me, our graphic designer is nudging my manager, pointing and laughing at the name of the song on my music console: "Gang Bang Anywhere."

We go off to lunch, have normal coworker banter, and come back to the office. When I get back to my desk, our graphic designer says something like "Gang bang?" to me, and I burst out laughing. Apparently everyone in the car was aware of what was being played, even though the volume was turned all the way down.

None of it really bothered me. I think some of this alludes to the question of how much of your whole self are you trying to bring to work, especially as a minority. It's something that we all struggle with in corporate America.

What are you reading right now? Any book recommendations?

Right now, I'm reading *The 4-Hour Workweek* by Tim Ferriss. I just started, so I don't have much of an opinion on the book yet. I pretty much read nonfiction exclusively. Here's a list of books that I recommend:

Product Management:
- *The Lean Startup* by Eric Ries
- *Cracking the PM Interview* by Gayle McDowell
- *Lean Analytics* by Alistair Croll and Ben Yoskovitz
- *The Innovator's Dilemma* by Clayton Christensen

Other:
- *Think Like a Programmer* by V. Anton Spraul
- *There Was a Country* by Chinua Achebe
- *Half of a Yellow Sun* by Chimamanda Adichie
- *Influence* by Robert Cialdini
- *Outliers* by Malcolm Gladwell
- *The Last Lecture* by Randy Pausch and Jeffrey Zaslow
- *Islam* by Karen Armstrong

What's the next move after this?

Super short-term? Keep promoting this book. Beyond that? To be determined. As I said before, I really enjoy my current job; I'm still learning daily, so that keeps me happy. In addition to this book, I've been working on some other projects that I think show promise.

Those who know me know my part of my goal has always been serial entrepreneurship, so that's still part of the plan. I'm just putting all the right things in place first.

If you could give your pre-B-School self advice, what would it be?

There are a few things I would tell myself. The first, and probably most important thing, would be not to go in the first place. Your classes will do a good job of teaching some of what you need to succeed as a business owner, but you're not going to learn everything unless you jump in and do it yourself. Going to business school hedges your bets, almost certainly resulting in a reduced commitment in your entrepreneurship goals.

My second piece of advice is to stay focused. You've seen this response from a number of the interviews, right? My friends were not lying. Every day, there's a different special event, large conference, company happy hour, corporate sponsored lunch, etc. If you're on a less traveled path, such as off-campus tech product management, you're going to start feeling an intense sense of "Fear of Missing Out" (FOMO). Imagine your classmates dressing up in suits every day for months, practicing for interviews, going to corporate sessions, and eventually getting internships and full time offers, while you're going to class and waiting for your turn. Some days, it's hard to manage.

The last thing I'd say is to get out of the business school bubble sometimes. A full-time business school program allows you to live like nothing else exists except school, classmates, and your eventual job. The students in programs at the other schools on campus are doing amazing things. The town or city surrounding you has a great depth of opportunities where you can test your skills. Don't restrict yourself to your classmates.

If you could give yourself advice back when you were about to graduate, what would it be?

1. Living close to work is one of the best decisions I've ever made. You'd be surprised how much not having to sit in traffic helps your overall happiness.
2. Make time for yourself post school. If you organize your days well, you'll find yourself with a respectable amount of free time that you can use for whatever you want. You may even write a book.
3. Don't skip exercise. Being in good health helps you perform better.
4. Get a job that will exercise the specific skills you want to get stronger on. Don't just pick something because you'll get paid a lot. If you're good at what you do, you'll find a way to make it work.
5. Think of yourself as a business. Capitalism is the name of the game in our society these days, and if you want to be "successful," you should see yourself as an active participant in this game. Work on your personal brand, just like a company would.
6. Fire people (or companies) who aren't adding value to your life.
7. Companies fire people all the time—don't get comfortable. Do what's best for yourself.
8. Always negotiate your offer.
9. Humble yourself. There's much to learn from just listening.

Was it worth it?

I hate the answer I'm about to give, but I don't know. I won't be able to answer that for another 10 years. Everything I do now, I could have done before my MBA. All of my potential corporate trajectories could have been achieved without business school because of the intense belief and determination I have in myself.

My faith isn't isolated to just my own abilities though. I truly believe that many of my classmates will go on to do great things (and make a bunch of money in the process). When I need help with my ideas, this will be my network and support system to get my ideas off of the ground. It will just take some time.

If anyone tells you a definitive yes or no without understanding your situation and motivations when you ask them about going to business school, they're giving you bad advice. The real answer is always, "It depends."

So there you have it. The graduates have spoken and given you their innermost thoughts. There were quite a few different opinions given here, so you may come off wondering, "What am I supposed to take from all of this?" While you know exactly what's best for you, I can offer some of my own thoughts.

For the consultants: Make sure you hustle to get the projects that you want. You want projects that add skills you're looking for and get you into industries that you want to be in. Don't just accept whatever project is put in front of you; make sure the partner you're working under knows what lane you would like to get into. This is the easiest way to transition into a good fit once your consulting career is over (if you indeed want to leave consulting). You had to put together a story just to get into business school; this story didn't end when you graduated. Having a plan can only help you from here on out.

For the marketers: Keep your notes from your marketing classes! I promise you there'll be a time when you'll ask yourself, "Didn't I learn this in school?" It's a gratifying experience to be able to pull out a notebook for reference. Every business, regardless of size, needs a marketing expert. The skills you acquire in your first job out of school make you valuable to smaller companies that need a marketing presence. That's an easier path to a director role that you can utilize to move ahead in the future with other employers.

For the finance folks: It's especially important to find a firm whose culture fits your style in this field. You'll probably be working more hours than your classmates. Do you want to spend these hours with people you don't mesh with? I know a lot of you may think you'll be in your position and company for years, but that doesn't happen often.

For the general managers: Push for an international stint as soon as you can. If you're working for a large multinational company, they can afford it. Take advantage of that development program. Learning the business side of another culture on some else's dime is always a good idea.

For the product managers: Absorb as much content as you possibly can inside and outside your specific product lane. Your product is in a constant market-share battle with its competitors, and you can learn much about how other products compete in their relative areas. The strategic moves of others can seem subtle and inconsequential to a casual observer, but many times, they have a large impact on the welfare of a product. It's always better to learn from someone else's mistakes.

For everyone: If you ask someone whether you should go to business school and they answer with an absolute yes or no, you're getting bad advice. Everyone's situation is exclusive and special to him or herself.

At the beginning of this book, I said you shouldn't get an MBA if you don't have a plan. I was dead serious about that. I know so many people who thought that the degree was going to free them of their corporate chains, only to find out that it's the same damn thing a year post school. Work is work, especially if you work for a large corporation. You're not going to escape that unless you blaze your own path.

You can be very successful without obtaining an MBA. By passing on the opportunity, you don't forego two years of salary (for a full-time program), and you don't have to take on $100K+ in debt. Pretty sweet deal, right? Please do the math before you send that deposit in.

On the other hand, the MBA can help fast-track your progress, especially if you're trying to switch careers or find a symbol that gives you credibility. Some industries are harder than others to transition into. They take a lot of networking that you wouldn't have access to without some sort of existing structure that facilitates it. MBA programs have these types of networking sessions every day.

If you have it planned out and you're ready to empty your pockets, take the leap. As you read previously, many people get a significant salary increase after business school. To be 100 percent honest, even people who don't really know what they want somehow get paid a lot of money to figure that out the first few years after school.

Given both of these sides, it's still clear that you have to assess your own situation and do what's best for yourself. I'd suggest that you really figure out what types of activities make you happy and move from there. If there are post-MBA roles that fit these profiles, then you may want to go for it.

Either way, you will never receive the success you're looking for unless you figure out what you want in the first place.

For more advice and info, check out http://lifeafterschool.co.

Made in the USA
Las Vegas, NV
11 December 2020